Dreaming in Church

Dreaming in Church

Dream Work as a Spiritual Practice for Christians

Geoff Nelson

WIPF & STOCK · Eugene, Oregon

Dreaming in Church
Dream Work as a Spiritual Practice for Christians

Wipf & Stock
An Imprint of Wipf and Stock Publishers
199 W. 8th Ave., Suite 3
Eugene, OR 97401

www.wipfandstock.com

PAPERBACK ISBN: 978-1-4982-3424-5
HARDCOVER ISBN: 978-1-4982-3426-9

Manufactured in the U.S.A.

This book is dedicated to my wife, Kim Romig, whose support and encouragement over the years have been invaluable.

Contents

Preface

This book offers a look into the fascinating world of dreams and dreaming. If you are interested in working with your dreams to reach a deeper understanding of yourself and the messages your dreams bring, this book contains guidelines on how to proceed. If you are seeking to deepen your religious or spiritual life, this book will give you specific suggestions for using your dreams in your spiritual life. I have written this book with three general audiences in mind: spiritual seekers from any tradition, Christian laypeople interested in their dreams, and Christian leaders, pastors, and teachers who are interested in leading people into the world of spirit as accessed through dreams. I'm a retired pastor, and this book reflects a pastoral approach to using dreams. It includes elements of psychology, myth and legend, biblical studies, etc., but the basic perspective is that of a pastor of a Protestant Christian church who seeks to lead people into a deeper understanding of themselves and of the workings of God's Holy Spirit.

The first group of anticipated readers of this book is spiritual seekers of any or no faith tradition who have an interest in dreams. Spiritual seekers will find help here, particularly if they are open to tending to their dreams in a group setting. Dreams have been a major focus in the religious quests of human beings for as far back as we have records, in virtually every culture and religious tradition. All humans dream, whether we recall our dreams or not. This book provides a general introduction to dreams and dreaming, discusses the significance of characters and activities in dreams, offers techniques for working with dreams, and discusses the advantages of dream work for spiritual seekers. Readers who are not Christian might wish to skip certain sections, such as the biblical and Christian historical background provided in chapters 2, 5, and 6. The discussion of spirituality in chapter 7, however, will be of interest to all spiritual seekers even though it is focused on spiritual practices within the Christian tradition. All of the discussion of dream characters and of the techniques and challenges of working with dreams provided in chapters 8 through 10 will be helpful for anyone interested in dreams.

The second group of anticipated readers is laypeople in the Christian church who have an interest in dreams. This book will be of particular interest to church members who are interested in learning about the specific help their dreams might provide to their spiritual lives. The biblical and historical portions of this book will help ground Christians in the use of dreams in the Bible and Christian history; they will find that they are in good company as they seek to know themselves and God more deeply through their dreams. The material in the book on background and techniques will be helpful as well. The connection between the world of dreams and the waking world is closely related to the religious practices of prayer and meditation, and the Christian tradition has great resources on these practices to offer the modern world.

The third anticipated audience is Christian pastors and lay leaders who are seeking a deeper understanding of dreams to assist them in their teaching, preaching, and leading. Dreams offer an excellent way to enhance our knowledge of ourselves and God. Dreams offer ready access to the world of spirit, and any leader familiar with the language of dreams will be able to assist others to know themselves and God better through their dreams. This book provides specific background, tools, and ideas for leaders to use with both individuals and groups who are working with their dreams. I focus on working with dreams in dream groups, and the composition and functioning of dream groups are addressed in some detail in the book. My perspective is that of a Presbyterian pastor working to help his congregation, and because of this my experiences with dreams will be helpful to teachers, small group leaders, and others in church leadership roles who are considering or are already using dreams in their work with others.

The final chapters of the book apply to anyone who hopes to pursue working with their own dreams. I offer suggestions for getting started and address particular challenges that arise in dream work. Dream work is not for everyone, so I discuss certain aspects of dream work that should be considered before deciding to pursue the meanings of one's dreams. For those seriously interested in moving to the next step and beginning to work with their dreams, specific instructions and references are provided. I include a discussion of how to use dreams in one's spiritual life.

I'd like to offer a word about the dreams described in this book. For reasons of confidentiality, I have changed the names in all dreams that name people. Many of the dreams used are my own dreams, some of which have been worked in various groups that I have participated in. I have also made my own dreams as "anonymous" as possible, changing the names and any other identifying characteristics in the dreams. When using the dreams of dream group members, I have secured permission from the dreamer and have also changed names or other details in such a way as to protect confidentiality without harming the integrity of the dream itself.

I have used two words in this preface to describe what is done with dreams by individuals or by dream groups. These words are *tend* and *work*. Later in the book I will also refer to *playing* with dreams. The use of these verbs is meant to highlight the different ways dreams can be learned from and used as guidance, inspiration, warnings, etc. Working with our dreams implies a more strenuous attitude towards our dreams, a more serious approach. This attitude may be appropriate in some situations. Tending to our dreams implies a more relaxed attitude toward our dreams, seeing them as phenomena that accompany us on our life journey but not, perhaps, as having to be totally understood or plumbed for their meaning. Playing with our dreams is the most lighthearted approach of the three outlined here. What kind of fun can we have with our dreams; how can we enjoy them and even laugh at and with them? These three words—work, tend, and play—are the ones used most often in this book to describe the activity of using our dreams as aids in our spiritual life. These three words, and the attitudes behind them, are not the only ways one can approach dreams, but they cover the general approach used in this book.

I offer various interpretations of particular dream narratives throughout this book. There are no doubt other interpretations that can be given to any of these dreams. Indeed, my experience has been that a person may work the same dream a month or a year later and get a different interpretation or understanding from it. That is part of the nature of dreams and of dreamers' changing life circumstances. But the interpretations and understandings given in the examples here are the ones that made the most sense to the dreamer at the time the dream work was done and that were followed up on in ways that benefited the dreamer. What counts in dream work is what use we can make of our dreams. There is more to our dreams than we may understand at any given moment. But, the dreamer can gain something from what he or she knows now about the dream without having to fully understand all the elements and all the depths of the dream.

It is my fervent hope that readers of this book will gain more insight, inspiration, and guidance from their dreams than they have ever had before. I trust many will discover the gift of dreams and dreaming that I believe God has given to each of us.

Acknowledgments

Without the support and encouragement of three communities, this book would not exist. The faculty, staff, and fellow students of the Diploma in the Art of Spiritual Direction program at San Francisco Theological Seminary provided the education, reflection, and criticism that trained me as a spiritual director and provided the container into which I put my work with dreams. The members of the International Association for the Study of Dreams have been the most encouraging and generous people I have ever worked with. And, the congregation and leaders of Whittier Presbyterian Church gave me the time, space, and encouragement to write the first draft. My deepest gratitude to these three communities.

Introduction

W hy did God create us as dreaming creatures? What is the purpose of those nightly stories that entertain, surprise, and baffle us, all at the same time? What can we learn from these experiences? How can our faith grow from them? How might God use our dreams to help us become better people?

> *I dream I'm back in Utah, in the hilly area up east of Highland, at what at first seems to be the old American Fork church manse where I had lived with my first wife, but when I go down into the basement I find that it spreads out towards the east with three or four more rooms. My current parents-in-law are there with my wife and children. As I explore the downstairs rooms, I find children of the current pastor in the rooms.*[1]

This dream was a powerful dream that woke me up in the night, and I did my usual work and prayer with it that morning and then carried it around with me for a few weeks, later taking it to my spiritual director. It became one of the most powerful dreams of my life, opening the way for me to make some significant life changes. Those changes resulted in further education and the expansion of my career and ministry into the area of dreams and dream work that this book is all about. I will work this dream later in this chapter as an example of how dreams can bring insights into one's life.

Why should we use dreams in the church? Those who are new to dream work might not see the potential benefit to tending in church to dreams such as the one described above. But those who have already had

---

1. All italicized block quotes in this book are dream narratives of the author or of dreamers he has worked with in dream groups.

some experience working with their own dreams might be eager to know more. How might our dreams help us in our lives of faith? This is the big question behind this book. This question is rooted in my personal history.

I was raised in the Presbyterian Church, baptized and confirmed in my local church. Then, through my college years, I hung on by my fingernails to the sense of meaning and purpose that I felt the church held for me. During the late 1960s, like so many youth of the time, I got involved with drugs and for a short while adopted the "hippie lifestyle," which for me included protesting against the war, changing my academic focus several times, and eventually dropping out of college before completing my degree work. A part of this spiritual journey included becoming a conscientious objector to war in general, prompted by the ambiguities of the Vietnam War. That required two years of alternative service instead of military service, so I spent two years working with the Salvation Army, doing drug rehabilitation work in residential programs for youth. My faith in Christ, the Bible, and ultimately the church helped me through these formative years and eventually pointed me in the direction of ordained ministry in the church of my youth, the Presbyterian Church.

Alas, I have no recall of dreams in this earlier part of my life. There were no dreams that stayed with me for years, no recurring dreams that seemed to press for resolution of some inner turmoil, no traumas from my childhood that needed therapy. But I did find my experiences with psychedelic drugs fascinating, and they opened me up to the spiritualities that were becoming popular then, along with drug use and the counter-cultural experiences that were part of many people's lives at the time. As I shifted from drug user to drug rehab counselor, I realized I had some further growing up to do, much of which involved inner work. My drug rehab work consisted of spending hours each week leading group therapy sessions that were very informal and were tailored to the particular program I was involved in. I ended up spending six years doing this kind of work, four years full-time and two years part-time, while I finished my undergraduate schooling. I was deeply moved and inspired by the simple psychology used in the program.

By the time I left the Salvation Army program in the mid-1970s, I'd participated in thousands of hours of this type of group therapy. I knew its value and saw the way it helped young people change their lives. I was looking for a way to bridge theology and psychology, but I was not interested in going into the world of therapy, even though at the time many churches were becoming involved in therapy and counseling programs and many clergy were abandoning parish ministry for counseling. I was still too interested in theology and church work to be very open to those career options. So I entered seminary, looking for connections between theology and psychology. I thought that the early fathers and mothers of the Christian church, those who went out to the deserts and wildernesses of the early Christian world, might have some insight into the psychological aspects of the Christian faith.

In my first semester at San Francisco Theological Seminary, the only course I could find that came anywhere near my desire to study the junction of theology and psychology was a course in Jung and theology offered by the Jesuit School of Theology in Berkeley. This focused upon the work of the Swiss psychologist Carl G. Jung, whose work dealt with religious issues. The class and the readings pertained almost exclusively to the work of Jung and his views of religion. The course gave me a good introduction to the psychology of Jung, but it was weak on the theological aspects. My opinion was prejudiced by the tremendous excitement I felt in learning about the theology of Paul Tillich, Dietrich Bonhoeffer, and particularly Karl Barth, all of which I was being introduced to in the required introduction to Reformed theology course I was taking concurrently with the Jung course. That excitement over the study of theology lasted the rest of my time in seminary.

After taking the Jung course, I began keeping track of my dreams. I had learned that one of the characteristics of analytical psychology (the branch of psychology that follows Jung and his principles) is the recognition of the importance of dreams. Every morning when I woke up I made some brief notes about my dreams in a spiral-bound notebook and dated them. I did this for several months, and then over the summer break between my first and second years of seminary I devised a prayer routine incorporating my dreams. This routine is essentially the same one I have followed to this day.

My daily prayer routine consists of recording the memories and notes I have of my dreams, doing a rudimentary interpretation of them (depending on how much time I have), and then formulating and writing down a prayer for the day, often using the material from my dreams or associations with that material to inform the prayer. In later years, when I was introduced to the practice of lectio divina, which is a traditional Christian prayer practice, I realized I had been doing a kind of lectio with my dreams.

Lectio divina is a particular way of praying with the Bible. This routine can also be applied to other forms of literature, to music, to artwork, to movies, etc. In doing lectio divina, ask yourself the following questions as you contemplate a text or other work:

1. What catches my attention?

2. Why did this attract my attention?

3. What might God be saying to me through this process? Or, how might this affect my prayer life?

In working with a dream using this process, I ask these questions:

1. What do I recall of the dream?

2. Why did this dream come to me at this time and place in my life?

3. What does God call me to do and be today, based on this dream as well as the various experiences of yesterday and my schedule of activities for today?

This has been my daily prayer routine over the past thirty-some years since I finished seminary, and the resulting integration of my dreams into my waking life and my prayer life has been a great blessing to me.[2]

After I finished seminary, I was ordained a Presbyterian minister and began working in my first congregation, a church in a small town in Utah. Since that time, and even now in my retirement, I continue to incorporate my dreams in my daily prayer practice. Every now and then over the years I have run across a book on dreams that looks like it might be helpful to me in modifying my prayer routine, but none of the books I have read have ever led me to change what I do in my daily prayers. Over time, I have read books about the early fathers and mothers of Christianity, learned a variety of prayer and spiritual practices, and attended a variety of retreats, workshops, and conferences having to do with church leadership, but nothing ever touched me deeply enough to change my prayer routine from the one I adopted in seminary that incorporates my dreams.

I left seminary thinking I would serve in a local church for three to five years and then return to school to get a doctorate in theology or historical theology. My plans were changed by my divorce and other events, but through it all I kept track of my dreams and maintained my personal prayer routine. Like many other mainline Protestant ministers, I pursued continuing education in areas that would benefit my ministry in my local church. During the last fifteen or so years of my professional ministry, I was

2. See a more detailed discussion of lectio divina and dream work in chapter 7.

involved in church redevelopment. My interior life continued to be fed and nourished by my personal daily prayer routine in which I incorporated my dreams into my prayers.

I also sought out retreats and workshops on prayer and other spiritual practices. One of my other desires in seminary, besides finding ways to connect psychology and theology, was to root my external activities in prayer. My decision to be a conscientious objector during the Vietnam War was a response in faith to the situation I saw around me. I was briefly involved in anti-war activities before I went to work in the drug rehabilitation program described above. I knew from personal experience as well as from observation that one cannot be involved in intense external or worldly affairs without a deep life of prayer, and I felt this applied to pastoral ministry. I remember hearing it said of Martin Luther that he had so much work to do each day that he couldn't possibly do it without an hour or two of prayer each morning. That became a model for me, and I never felt embarrassed or guilty about following my daily prayer routine. One particularly helpful spiritual practice that I found was spiritual direction, which is meeting regularly with a qualified person to talk over my life in the spirit, my life with God. This is a practice that I've maintained for over twenty years now, and I have received training to certify myself as a spiritual director. But, it has only been in the last few years that I have introduced my prayer experiences with dreams into my sessions with my spiritual director. That has made a great difference in my spiritual life, enabling me to integrate on deeper levels my waking life and my dreaming life.

One of the areas that I explored beginning in the year 2000 was retreat work and leadership, which I was drawn to because I felt I had some gifts and talents to offer. I became involved as a preacher and small group leader in a program called Companions on the Inner Way, which offers guided retreats grounded in the Christian tradition. As I became increasingly involved with that program, I paid attention to the language and experience of prayer as we talked and practiced various prayer and spirituality techniques. I felt there were similarities between that language and those experiences and my experiences with my dreams. At one retreat I asked the leaders if I could take an hour one afternoon during the retreat to talk to the group about my interest in dreams, in case anyone attending the retreat might be interested. The arrangements were made, and to my amazement there was standing room only at the lecture I gave. That was the first experience I had of sharing my interest in and practice with dreams. That event turned into the beginning of a year-long process during which I discerned that I should go back to school and get an academic grounding for my interest in dreams and spirituality.

At about this time, one of my own dreams spoke powerfully to me, the one that opens this introduction. This was a dream I had in 2003 that I later titled "Deeper American Fork House." I repeat below the excerpt from what was actually a longer dream. Many other parts of this dream related to issues in my waking life at the time, but I did not seize upon and follow them in such a dramatic fashion as I did this particular part of the dream. This part of the dream became a theme for me, a metaphor for the studies and work I undertook over the next several years. Following the narrative is background material to help this part of my dream be understandable to anyone. Then I describe some of the "work" I did with this dream, the type of dream work that is integral to my practice of using dreams in church groups. Here is the significant part of the dream:

> I dream I'm back in Utah, in the hilly area up east of Highland, at what at first seems to be the old American Fork church manse where I had lived with my first wife, but when I go down into the basement I find that it spreads out towards the east with three or four more rooms. My current parents-in-law are there with my wife and children. As I explore the downstairs rooms, I find children of the current pastor in the rooms.

Background to this portion of the dream:

1. The first church I served was Community Presbyterian Church in American Fork, Utah, a small town about thirty miles south of Salt Lake City, Utah. I was there from 1977 to 1985.

2. Highland is the name of a community to the north of American Fork.

3. A manse is usually a house owned by a local church and provided to the pastor during his or her stay as pastor of that church. Such was the case while I was pastor of this church in Utah.

This dream led me to see that I was deepening my sense of call from God— or was being given the opportunity to do so. I took this from the images in the dream of the basement of the house going back farther and deeper than it did in reality. Paying attention to the mix of characters in the dream from my life in the 1980s and in 2003, I looked for meaning that might speak to me in 2003. The image of a basement or cellar is an image for one's unconscious, for the deeper parts of one's self, perhaps an image for the soul. This image spoke most strongly to me. I was about to enter the phase of my life that I later titled "The Deepening," referring to the deepening of my call from God. This title came specifically from this part of this dream, from the image of an extended or deeper basement with more rooms and spaces in it than when I had lived in it. In some methods of dream interpretation, Jungian in particular, a house in a dream represents the dreamer him or herself. The deepening of the underground part of the house that may have represented me seemed a clear message to deepen that part of myself related to my work and my theological training. This was a very powerful dream, and some other aspects of it that related to my daily waking life at the time were helpful to me as well. But it was the "vision" of a deeper interior life that really captured my attention and was very helpful in my articulating what the next few years of my life would be like. It took about eight to ten weeks for me to formulate the changes in my life I would make as a consequence of this dream.

During the discernment process that I went through after having this dream, I discovered that there is a whole movement of people interested in using their dreams to help them discover deeper things about themselves and the world around them. Some of the people in this movement are religious; of these, some are Christian and some are New Age seekers. Others are scientists who do not value dreams for religious purposes. Many members of this movement belong to the International Association for the Study of Dreams (IASD). I have become active in this group and enjoy the highly stimulating workshops, seminars, and presentations about dreams at the annual conferences of the IASD. I have even been involved in organizing a regional chapter of the IASD in Southern California. But, I'm getting ahead of the story.

In the discernment process that resulted from my dream, I had a consultation with Rev. Dr. Jeremy Taylor, a well-known dream worker with over forty years of experience working with dreams. He said a number of things to me that catalyzed my discernment process. One of these was, "Only you know the meaning of your dreams." I realized in the succeeding months that I'd read that phrase before, but for whatever reason I'd not been able to hear it the way I heard it from Taylor that day. My discernment led me into several study and training programs. I am now a labyrinth facilitator, certified by the Veriditas organization out of San Francisco, and I have also received the Diploma in the Art of Spiritual Direction from San Francisco Theological Seminary. I received the Doctor of Ministry (DMin) degree from the Graduate Theological Foundation in South Bend, Indiana, and my project for this program involved leading dream groups in churches. Some of the material from that doctoral work appears in this book, and many of the examples and illustrations come out of that experience and from participants in the dream groups that were part of the project.

My explorations and training in these various areas of spirituality have further reinforced my experience that dreams are a valuable tool in our total lives, but I also believe that they are particularly helpful in our religious lives. That is the argument I make in this book. I continue to be involved in dream groups, and I continue to find that working with dreams is of great value to those who participate in the groups. The potential for deepened spirituality through tending to our dreams exists for all people of whatever faith, even for those of no faith. Dreams offer a deeper connection with the life of the Holy Spirit, and this can benefit not only the person leading such a life but also those around him or her. The life of the Christian church has been guided by the Holy Spirit throughout its two millennia of existence. The use of dreams in the Christian church offers yet another way for individuals to access that spirit and to revitalize their own lives and the life of the church around them. This book is dedicated to that end, to revitalizing Christians and the Christian church through working with our nightly dreams.

1

Overview of Dreams and Dreaming

*I'm visiting my old friend John in his apartment on the top floor
of a beachfront building. There are large picture windows on both
walls of the corner where I'm sitting. It's stormy outside, with cloudy
weather and maybe rain. Lightning strikes the building and lights up
the room, especially the window frames, and I have a strong tingling
feeling. I decide to move away from the windows in case it happens
again. John stays where he is. I'm starting to tell him what the power
company recommends if the power goes out when another much
larger and more powerful lightning strike hits. This time I'm totally
blinded by the flash and my body feels a strong shock, as though from
an electrical outlet. When it is over I try to ask John if he is okay, but
I seem semi-paralyzed and am not able to talk clearly. This is a very
powerful experience during the dream, with strong sensations like a
real electrical shock. I awaken, and both my arms are tingling from
my having slept on them in such a way that the blood flow has been
restricted—they are "asleep."*

I took this dream to my dream group because I was curious about the
physical effects on me in the dream. Could they be explained by the fact
that my sleeping position had constricted the blood flow to my arms? If that
were the case, this dream could be consigned to the bin of dreams caused
by some external stimulus.

By the time I had this dream, I'd worked with my dreams for nearly
thirty years and knew there was more to this dream than the way I'd been
sleeping, though my sleep position had had an influence. But in the case of
this particular dream, it was the events following the working of the dream
that made the dream stand out for me. The group with whom I shared the
dream asked me a number of questions about it, particularly about the

other character, my friend John. We spent some time on various aspects of the dream, but I left the group that night having made a commitment that I would contact John and see how he was doing. To my amazement, when I contacted him the next day he told me of two events that had taken place in his life recently that had been very painful. He had been downsized out of his job and his partner's mother had been very ill. Neither of those events was referenced directly in the dream, but the fact that I dreamt of two lightning strikes, two powerful experiences, in John's house around the time of these two actual events in his life made me realize there was more to this dream than I or even the others in the dream group had realized. The group was moved by this story when I shared it with them in our next meeting.

Dreams have fascinated human beings since before the beginning of history. These strange and wonderful stories that come when we are sleeping can have powerful effects upon us—they can change our lives and even change history. Or, they can seem so silly and nonsensical that we simply ignore them or attribute them to some insignificant external effect, such as the popular explanation that dreams result solely from external stimuli such as something we ate or, as in the above case, a physical sensation in our body. I argue throughout this book that dreams can be both powerful and nonsensical but that we will not know the difference unless we begin to pay attention to them.

What are the dreams that I'm talking about here? The dreams I focus upon in this book are those occurrences associated with sleep—not our hopes and desires; not our aspirations and fantasies; not our abstract states of mind or reveries, like daydreams; not a dream man or dream woman who is the ideal, personalityless creation of our own desires; not a dream job, dream vacation, etc.; not the verb *dreaming* in the sense of conceiving of a plan, imagining, or fancying. All these meanings associated with the word *dream* may influence or be related to our nightly sleep-related dreams, but they are not what this book focuses upon. I am most interested in the "little movies" that happen while we are asleep, the dreams that mix up the events, characters, actions, and emotions of our waking lives in such a way that they offer us new and creative ways to address the challenges of our lives.

This chapter offers a general introduction to dreams and dreaming as a prelude to the main content of the book. The chapter has three sections addressing the following topics: the characteristics of dreams and dreaming, the physiology of dreaming, and the democracy of dreaming.

Characteristics of Dreams and Dreaming

> The stage of sleep usually associated with dreaming may have evolved in mammals about 130 million years ago. Everyone dreams and in an average lifetime, we will spend about 5 to 6 years dreaming. This is a huge chunk of our life, and a conservative estimate is that more than 95% of all dream mentation is completely unremembered.
>
> —Robert L. Van de Castle, *Our Dreaming Mind*

Dreams have played a surprisingly active role in human civilization, influencing the arts and sciences, religion, and history. It is truly a wonder that dreams are not given more credibility in Western culture when one looks at the variety of contributions that dreams have made. Many authors have compiled lists of the important contributions dreams have made over the centuries.[1] This is my own list of the top five historical events in which dreams played an important role:

- George Eastman, founder of Eastman Kodak Company, dreamt of a way to produce film for color movies as well as a plan for how to market it. He wired his production chief the dream's details and told him to get started.

- German chemist Friedrich August Kekulé figured out the structure of the benzene ring through a dream of a snake biting its tail. This became the foundation of organic chemistry.

- Albert Einstein, at age fourteen, had a dream that led to his formulation of the theory of relativity.

- George Frideric Handel first heard the last movements of his musical masterpiece, *The Messiah,* in a dream.

- American inventor Elias Howe had a dream that contributed to the invention of the sewing machine. He dreamt he was being chased by natives in a jungle and that the spears they were carrying had holes in the tips.

Other discoveries attributed to dreams include insulin, oil wells, and math formulas. Dreams have predicted national and international tragedies, from the assassination of Abraham Lincoln to the beginning of World War

---

1. An excellent list of the contributions of dreams throughout history can be found in Van de Castle, *Our Dreaming Mind.*

I. I will look at the role of dreams in religion, in particular in Christianity, in chapters 5 and 6.

What is a dream? In moving from dreaming to the dream itself, I find the following distinction made by Jorge Luis Borges helpful:

> Now the study of dreams presents a special difficulty: the fact that we cannot examine dreams directly. We can only examine or talk about the recollection of dreams. Possibly the recollection of dreams does not correspond directly to them. A great writer of the 17th century, Sir Thomas Brown, thought that our recollection of dreams was much poorer than the splendid reality of them. Others, on the other hand, think that we improve our dreams, that is, if we think that dreams are works of fiction (and I believe so) we will probably continue to imagine as we wake up and later when we tell about our dreams.[2]

The following definition of dreams from the 1984 book *Dreams and Spiritual Growth* by Savary, Berne, and Williams gives a more complete picture of what a dream is:

> A night dream is a spontaneous symbolic experience lived out in the inner world during sleep. Such dreams are composed of a series of images, actions, thoughts, words, and feelings over which we seem to have little or no conscious control. The people, places, and things of our dreams can sometimes be related to remembered life experiences or images that remain in our memory, but often they seem to come from sources to which we have little or no conscious access.[3]

Carl Jung, on the other hand, emphasizes the role of the dreamer in interpreting the universal symbols found in dreams: "[I treat] the dream . . . as a direct, personal, and meaningful communication to the dreamer—a communication that uses the symbols common to all mankind, but that uses them on every occasion in an entirely individual way that can be interpreted only by an entirely individual 'key.'"[4]

The bottom line is that there is no universally accepted definition of a dream, which gives us some personal freedom in understanding what a dream is. Since all people dream, I hope much of the material throughout

---

2. Jorge Luis Borges, as quoted in Hobson, *The Dreaming Brain*, 225.

3. Savary et al., *Dreams and Spiritual Growth*, 4.

4. Jung, *Man and His Symbols*, 13.

this book will provoke responses of familiarity in the reader, a personal "aha, yes, I've experienced that."

Why do we dream? What purposes do dreams serve? Despite millennia of human dreaming and the more recent application of new scientific tools to the study of dreaming, no one really knows for sure. The next section on dreams and sleep physiology gives a brief description of the findings of cognitive neuroscience. First, though, I summarize below the points on which there is consensus related to particular elements of dreams and dreaming:

- We can identify and measure the effects on humans when dreaming does not take place.

- Our brains are as active when we are sleeping as when we are awake, sometimes slightly more active.

- Dreams and dreaming play a role in memory and learning. Dreams may, in their own unique language, bring up previous experiences but substitute current characters or situations to help us learn to cope with new conditions in our lives.

- Evolutionists say threat management helps determine who among us will survive. They note that dreams help us "rehearse" situations of threat so that when an actual threat occurs, we will have more resources for coping with it.

- Many, even most, of our dreams seem to reflect everyday events from our waking lives.

Scientific research reaffirms the wisdom in the adage "Sleep on it!"[5] Our nightly dreaming helps us manage our life in the waking world.

The dreams we experience can be classified in a variety of ways. Based on my personal experience, I categorize dreams as follows:

1. Dreams rehashing yesterday's events, feelings, etc.

   I dream of an earthquake and my stereo equipment falls over.

   This dream came to me the night after I had just rearranged the stereo equipment in my home study. The dream prompted me to realize the

---

5. This saying expresses the common experience that dreaming gives us insights into our daily life and any problems or decisions we may face. *Sleep On It* is also the title of an excellent book on dreaming by Janice Baylis.

stereo would not fare well in an earthquake, so I rearranged every-thing the next day. This dream and my subsequent action based upon it is an example of using material in a dream to make positive—often minor but sometimes major—changes in life. These kinds of dreams may reflect aspects of our activities from the day before that we have not paid sufficient attention to, which is related to "day residue," or material from our daily lives that finds its way into our dreams (this will be discussed in more detail in chapter 8). Even dreams such as these, as common and familiar as the dream material may be, can contain helpful insights.

2. Compensatory dreams

> *I dream of getting respect, praise, and adulation from an older woman with whom I work and whom I depend upon for support and encouragement.*

This dream came to me at a time when I was feeling particularly lonely and believed that no one was paying attention to me or to the work I was doing. It was clearly a compensatory dream, the kind of dream that helps our inner selves make up for something we may be lacking in our conscious lives. As another example, I sometimes have dreams of vacations or characters that I associate with vacations when I begin to get stressed or when a vacation is indeed approaching.

3. Recurring dreams

During my last year of seminary a classmate had recurring dreams of death and murder. These grew more and more violent and frightening as graduation drew near. This kind of dream, one that repeats itself, is a signal to the dreamer to pay attention to something in their life that they have been ignoring. In this dreamer's case, he had gone from high school right into college and from college right into seminary. He had never held a regular job. Though I did not understand it at the time, I've come to see how such dreams signify a death of part of one's self, a death of who one has been up to that point in one's life. In my classmate's case, he needed to die to the inexperienced and dependent person he had been up to that point in his life. He needed to make the shift to a mature adult who was able to hold down a job and manage all the responsibilities of an adult. Recurring dreams are ongoing scenes or predicaments that are dreamt on a repeating basis. These may reflect deeper concerns and indicate the need for therapy. An important point is that dreams about these kinds of deeper things only surface when one's soul or psyche feels it can deal with the issue. If recurring dreams are not addressed, they may turn into nightmares.

4. Nightmares

As in the above example, nightmares may be a variation of recurring dreams. Though disturbing, they can be a source of great help for us. These are concerns that need addressing; they will "knock on our door" until we let them in. As with recurring dreams, they only come when we are indeed ready to deal with them, but we must be willing to do the work involved in order to understand them.

5. Revelatory or highly memorable dreams

> *I dream I'm in a mental hospital or training center for developmentally disabled people. I begin to shuffle with a limping gait and to talk very simply. I hang around with everyone and seem to blend in very well, and none of the attendants seem to notice me. Then a tall guy comes along and befriends me. He seems to be either a graduate of this program or maybe some kind of trustee. He tells me I can go home with him, so I start to walk away with him. No one seems to notice or care. We walk along, and I'm really surprised at the gentleness and innocence of this guy.*

This dream was quite powerful, and I woke from it well before my alarm went off and never went back to sleep. In talking to my wife about it later, she pointed out that I was moving from one phase of my life into another and that the dream seemed to indicate that shift. Such highly memorable dreams may involve seeing a new way that things work, reaffirming your call or your worth as a person and the gifts you have, changing the direction of your life/career, etc. The biblical dreams of Jacob or of the two different Josephs in the Old and New Testaments belong in this category.

6. Lucid dreams

Lucid dreams seem to capture people's imagination because of the perception that the dreamer having a lucid dream can control the progress and outcome of the dream. I often hear this misconception in public discussions of dreams. In contrast, this is Jeremy Taylor's definition of this type of dream. H focuses simply on the awareness that one is having a dream:

> Any dream in the midst of which the dreamer has the clear thought "Oh! I get it! This is a *dream!*" is said to be "lucid." In a lucid dream, the dreamer recognizes more fully the true nature of the experience *as it is taking place*, instead of the far more common experience of discovering only upon awakening, "Oh, it was all a dream."[6]

I have had occasional lucid dreams, but not nearly as often as people who cultivate them. I admit to having a certain prejudice about lucid dreaming. My interest in dreams is to see what is being said to me either by my subconscious, my conscience, my greater self, or God. Thus, I am interested in what comes from a source other than my conscious mind. My prejudice about lucid dreaming is due to the fact that lucid dreamers often try to influence and manipulate their dreams for their own conscious benefit. I'm more interested in listening to my dreams, not in talking back to them during the dream itself. One image that helps me in my understanding of lucid dreaming is that of a sailor on the sea. The sailor does not control the sea but merely navigates upon the sea.[7] That image is a reminder that although we do not create the dreams or the world of dreams, we may have some choice in how we explore that world.

What might our dreams be telling us? Dreams tell us what is important in our daily lives, the things we might otherwise overlook. They may be telling us of things we feel but cannot yet name. They may "defuse" daily events, helping us process and resolve situations and experiences from our waking lives. They may help us solve problems or find alternatives to situations we face. Our dreams may show us the next step in our inner growth. I believe that we are the only ones who can decide for certain what our dreams mean. A variety of approaches and methods can help us do the work that is needed to determine the meaning of any particular dream. In my experience, dream groups offer the best way to work with dreams.

6. Taylor, *Where People Fly,* 201.
7. Waggoner, "Does the Sailor Control the Sea?"

There are a great number of theories about dreams and dreaming. Those of Sigmund Freud and Carl Jung are probably the best known.[8] The topic of theories about dreams is much larger than the scope of this book and will be only briefly addressed in chapter 4. Jung is much more friendly and open to religion than Freud is, and this book refers primarily to Jung's theories.

The process of recalling and praying about our dreams gives us a fuller picture of ourselves and the things going on around us, which can only deepen our spiritual life. Our dreams are not God speaking to us, though God can speak through our dreams. Our dreams do not contain the secret to our life, though they can reveal much about ourselves that we may not otherwise catch. Our dreams are a part of who we are, and thus they will benefit our spiritual life to the degree that we offer them to God, just as we offer to God the rest of our life.

The Physiology of Dreaming

The first known record of a dream is that of King Gudea of Sumeria, who ruled around 2200 BCE. In the 4000-plus years since then, dreams have been part of written history and the inquiry into human existence. The idea that dreams are caused by external physical stimuli, like what we eat or what happens to us in our waking world, is often mentioned. This has gone hand in hand with the idea that dreams come from the gods, the spirit world, or some other non-physical realm. Over the last few hundred years in the Western world, the intensity of the debate has increased as scientists have found ways to measure electrical and chemical actions in the body down to the level of the individual cell. The growth of science, and of the rational, materialistic worldview that has accompanied it, has caused a split in the world of dream research as well as in areas of faith and religion in

8. Modern work done on dreams must take into account the insights and theories of Freud and Jung. J. Allan Hobson, in his 1988 book *The Dreaming Brain,* focuses primarily on disproving the psychoanalytic theories of Freud and examining instead the physiological basis of dreaming. Robert L. Van de Castle, in his 1994 book *Our Dreaming Mind,* is also critical of Freud and leans more heavily on the work of Jung. Kelly Bulkeley, in *Visions of the Night* (1999) and *The Wondering Brain* (2005), gives thorough analyses and critiques of the work of both Freud and Jung, outlining the strengths and weaknesses of each. Morton Kelsey and John Sanford, both Episcopalian priests, rely heavily on the work of Jung in their writings on dreams but also consider the work of Freud, as is essentially the case for all recent books on dreams and dreaming.

general. In the academic world, this division can be categorized as the areas of religious studies and cognitive neuroscience.[9] In this book I focus upon the religious use of dreams, but I also address ways religion and science might find some common ground or at least better understand each other. This section looks briefly at the physiology of dreams and dreaming in order to introduce the reader to this aspect of the study of dreams.

Freud spent time studying the physiological aspects of dreams but eventually abandoned this pursuit, in part due to the inability of science to measure and observe the human body in the ways that would be needed for physiological studies. Today, however, we are much more fortunate; it is possible to pursue the study of dreams with a great deal of scientific evidence and insight because scientists are now able to measure the activity of the body while dreaming. In 1953, the discovery of Rapid Eye Movement (REM) opened up the study of the physiological aspects of dreams and dreaming.[10] In the more than sixty years since the discovery of REM sleep, the area of dream physiology has grown greatly.

There are four phases of sleep, each with different kinds of measurable brain waves. Sleep takes place in cycles of ninety minutes. Our dreams get longer in each cycle per sleep period, and the last cycle may have a REM period of up to forty minutes. This last cycle takes place just before waking, after a night of seven to nine hours of normal sleep. This is the period when most of the dreams we recall take place, just before waking in the morning (or whenever our normal period of sleep takes place). Sleep laboratories that trace subjects' REM have demonstrated that dreams may indeed last a long time, not just seconds as some—most notably Freud—had thought. Though I focus here on the REM stage of sleep, there are other general areas of sleep, as listed below.[11] The various types of waves listed below refer to the classifications given to the wave patterns in an electroencephalogram (EEG).

1. Waking, characterized by beta waves and alpha waves; the latter indicate a higher state of relaxation. Alpha waves are highlighted in various meditation techniques for reducing stress and other purposes.

2. REM phase, characterized by rapid eye movement and theta EEG waves. This is the phase most actively associated with dreams.

3. Delta phase with 20–50 percent delta waves.

9. Bulkeley, *The Wondering Brain*, 3.

10. Hobson, *The Dreaming Brain*, 123.

11. Van de Castle, *Our Dreaming Mind*, 232–34.

4. Delta phase with > 50 percent delta waves, also known as "dead sleep," the deepest period of sleep.

Both of the delta-wave sleep periods may include some dream activity, but it's rarely the kind of narrative dream activity that is associated with dreams that are recalled.

One of the most practical ways to use the research on REM and sleep cycle is in improving your dream recall. Dream recall can be an issue for those beginning to pay attention to their dreams, particularly in the early stages of learning the techniques of dream recall and dream study. Noticing when the REM periods occur in your sleep cycle can aid your recall. If you get a full night's sleep (more than seven hours), the last sixty to ninety minutes of sleep will be the most productive in terms of dreams. Since this is also normally the last period before waking, you will be more likely to recall dreams from that period. One of the techniques for learning to better recall your dreams is to plant the seed subconsciously, through the power of suggestion, that the period just before waking will be the most fruitful time for you. As you wake up, if you remember your planted suggestion you will be more likely to recall what was going on in your mind just before waking. Another way to do this, at the other end of the sleep session, is to focus on the first REM period, which happens 90 to 120 minutes after falling asleep. This may be another period when you might be able to recall dreams. By taking a large drink of water before going to bed, you likely will awaken about 90 to 120 minutes later to make a trip to the bathroom. This roughly coincides with the first REM period, and you may recall a dream as you wake up to go to the bathroom. More such techniques will be discussed in chapter 9, where I describe how to get started in the process of dream recall.

One aspect of dream physiology has to do with the concept of the left and right brains. Physiologists have tied dreams to specific parts of the brain itself, but I will simply describe the general ideas behind this approach. According to Robert J. Hoss:

> [The] "left brain" has been found to be more involved in understanding language, processing speech and reading, labeling things with words, and in linear logical thinking. . . . The right hemisphere, or "right brain," is more involved in processing non-verbal information (music, art, pattern recognition), forming associations and understanding what an object represents (as opposed to its name) and in visual understanding. It also detects and

interprets anomalies of experience, a process that is important in understanding the nature of dreams.[12]

The popular understanding of the difference between the two sides of the brain is that artists are right-brained people while engineers are left-brained people. This is an oversimplification, but the distinction is important for doing dream work as the dreamer needs to rely upon his or her right-brain characteristics. This is particularly difficult for those accustomed to relying primarily on their left-brain characteristics. For example, a participant in one of my dream groups struggled with much of his dream material. He'd been trained as an engineer, and his dream material just did not make sense to his engineer's mind. Yet, he kept bringing dreams to the group and seemed to have a hunger for whatever was happening for him in the group. One night, I stopped the flow of the group to explore and explain the right brain-left brain issue. It was an opportune time to get this man's attention. In his own logical way, he seemed to understand the different ways the brain or the mind worked and expressed his gratitude for having right and left brain function explained to him.

The results of contemporary physiological research on dreams can be difficult for non-scientists to assimilate, but I had an experience one day that helped me in this endeavor. My eleven-year-old son had many pieces of Legos in his room that constantly needed to be picked up. My imagination came up with the idea that our brains begin as a mass of something like jelly or, as my imagination saw it, small Lego pieces. As the complexity of the tasks required of us grows, more and more pieces are organized and more and more organic material is combined, while the brain learns to form new neural networks. Part of the function of dreams is to "preview" the new networks—or better, to begin to make the building blocks needed to learn a new task. Like Legos, the networks build whatever is needed.

One of the interesting aspects of dreaming and brain activity is the level of brain activity while we are asleep. Many believe that while we are sleeping our brain is at rest, but contemporary science enables us to know in detail how our brains are functioning while we are asleep. Surprisingly, certain parts of the brain are more active during dreaming than when we are awake, and the overall output of brain waves can reach levels during dreaming that exceed the total output of brain waves during waking activity. Far from resting during sleep, our brains continue to be active at similar levels to when we are awake.

12. Hoss, *Dream Language*, 40–41.

One influential theory of dreaming is the idea that dreams act like a garbage disposal, flushing out the unneeded material that our brains or minds accumulate during the day. Scientists Francis Crick and Graeme Mitchison adhere to this idea: "Attempting to remember one's dreams should perhaps not be encouraged, because such remembering may help to retain patterns of thought which are better forgotten. These are the very patterns the organism was attempting to damp down."[13] In other words, not everyone sees keeping track of one's dreams as valuable. That dreams might have spiritual significance or might offer us the ability to better understand ourselves is not given much credibility by the "garbage disposal" theorists. Jeremy Taylor critiques the work of those who consider dreams meaningless:

> The most serious problem with the work of Crick, Mitchison, and the rest of the laboratory researchers who assert that dreams are meaningless "garbage" is that they fail to recognize that the very process of sorting and "forgetting" on which they place so much emphasis is itself a model of the process of the generation and perception of meaning in human consciousness.[14]

As a pastor who has worked for decades with people seeking meaning in daily life and in the tragedies they experience, I believe that we are created to seek meaning in our lives. For me, religious faith is less fire insurance, designed to keep us out of hell, than it is a framework or container into which we can put or find meaning for our lives. I believe our dreams help us to do that in a way that provides greater insight than we generally realize.

The Democracy of Dreaming

One of the appeals of dreams to me is that they are universal—they happen to everyone. I like to call this "the democracy of dreaming," although the concept is not original to me, nor is it a recent one. As Synesius of Cyrene wrote over sixteen hundred years ago:

> But the dream is visible to the man who is worth five hundred *medimni*, and equally to the possessor of 300, to the teamster no less than to the peasant who tills the boundary land for a

---

13. Crick and Mitchison, "The Function of Dream Sleep," 114.
14. Taylor, *The Living Labyrinth*, 8.

livelihood, to the galley slave and the common laborer alike, to the exempted and to the payer of taxes.[15]

For me, the importance of the democracy of dreams is that dreams offer a method of self-analysis and growth that is available to everyone. Likewise, dreams are also available to everyone as a spiritual practice. One need not learn complex body postures or foreign languages or travel to some remote spot or pay to study a special technique. Our dreams provide a ready tool to assist us in spiritual growth. Having said that, I realize that dream language is like a foreign language for many people and that it often takes learning some special techniques to benefit from one's dreams. But the original material—the dreams themselves and the process of dreaming—is universal, there for everyone. As Van de Castle puts it, "The great feature about dreams is that you don't have to make an appointment; they'll come to you on a regular basis, and for free, and all they ask in return is that you pay attention to them."[16]

The experience of dreaming is universal; all humans do it. The language of dreams is also universal in that it is symbolic, not relying on any specific spoken language. I will look more closely at the language of dreams in chapter 4. This preliminary sketch of the realm of dreams has described the basic characteristics of dreaming and the basic physiological aspects of the dreaming process. The next chapter looks at working with dreams in the Christian church and in group settings.

15. Kelsey, *God, Dreams, and Revelation*, 247. Synesius lived from about 373 to 414 CE.
16. Van de Castle, *Our Dreaming Mind*, 335.

2

Dream Work in the Church

I dream I'm in a passenger jet airplane that flies down along the streets of a city between the tall buildings and finally lands on one of the streets. Several people get off the plane with me. There are crowds of people in the street, and just a couple of blocks away I see two large churches the size of cathedrals. They are painted all kinds of colors in patterns that look like stained glass.

This dream came to me at the very beginning of my process of deciding how and what to do with the last years of my career, especially in relation to my growing interest in working with dreams. The churches in this dream were beautiful, and they became for me symbols of what I wanted to do and where I wanted to go. I wanted to work in colorful, attractive churches and help people use their dreams to enrich their waking and spiritual lives. There are many symbols in this dream, each of which might bear deeper work, but it was the gorgeous, multicolored churches that spoke to me and helped inspire me to do the work that I pursued in the months following the dream.

What might be the value of dreams in the Christian church? Is there a possibility that dreams might add some color, some vibrancy, to the contemporary church? The last few decades have seen an increase in the use of various spiritual practices and disciplines drawn from the history of Christianity. Could dream work be considered of equal value to these traditional practices? Of particular relevance to the theme of this book, could dream groups provide new and meaningful types of experiences to believers?

In the Christian tradition, the religious community—the church—is supposed to be the place where people can experience God or the divine and share their faith experiences. It is where congregants are nourished, supported, and motivated to be sent out to serve God in the world. By *the church* I mean the local manifestation of the larger body. Each local Christian church provides a place where individuals' faith can find expression and be given opportunities to grow in community. This chapter will give some background on the relationship between the church and dreams, as well as on the ways in which churches aid people in channeling their religious drives—and sometimes get in the way of those religious drives.

Where does religion come from? Evidence of religion or religious impulses dates back long before written history. The cave paintings found in Europe, the first "written" or historical evidence of human communication, may well have been religious expressions. What is the source of this thirst for meaning, for a place in the cosmos, which for most of human history has taken form in religious practices and doctrines? According to Kelly Bulkeley,

> Religion can be seen as expressing a fundamental human need to answer questions about the ultimate nature of our lives. We humans need to find or create meanings, images, and values that can provide us with existential orientation. It is not concerned with churches, priests, or dogmas; rather it is concerned with seeking vital, trustworthy meanings that express our responses to these ultimate questions and concerns.[1]

Note that this definition refers to our need to find meaning in this world in our current lives. I believe dreams can be of great help to us in our search for a sense of meaning as it applies to our individual lives.

Some people view religion as "fire insurance." Religion provides the insurance we need against eternal fire (one of the traditional Christian images of hell). This is a view of religion that is more concerned with life after death than with the meaning found in this life. Both of these dynamics of faith—finding deeper meaning in our lives and protecting us after death—reflect aspects of the human condition, and all great religions address these concerns. In the Christian tradition, religion is a communal or group experience that has individual expressions and practices. Christians gather into communities to better live out their religious lives. For Protestant Christians of various denominations, this experience is essentially the same, although

1. Bulkeley, *Visions of the Night*, 71.

there are some minor variations in form and focus. For example, the constitution of the Presbyterian Church (U.S.A.), the denomination in which I'm an ordained minister, expresses the nature of the church as follows:

> The Church universal consists of all persons in every nation, together with their children, who profess faith in Jesus Christ as Lord and Savior and commit themselves to live in a fellowship under his rule.
>
> Since this whole company cannot meet together in one place to worship and to serve, it is reasonable that it should be divided into particular congregations. The particular church is, therefore, understood as a local expression of the universal Church.[2]

Though a specifically Presbyterian formulation, these sentiments can be found in similar form among other mainline Protestant churches.

This chapter addresses the interconnection of the church and dreams in five sections. First, I give some general background on dreams and dreaming, including specific information on Protestantism in relation to dreams and dreaming. The next section covers the history of resistance to working with dreams, which is rooted in the Bible and continues in some circles to the present day. The third section discusses the contributions that dreams and dreaming can make to the contemporary Christian church. The fourth is a discussion of the concept of the soul, specifically as it is related to dreams and the church. I conclude with a discussion of why dream work needs to have a structure around it, a container, such as that which the church can provide.

Dreams in the Church

I'm doing a funeral, maybe for a woman in the congregation or perhaps for a man. I know the church is supposed to be my current church, but it actually is entirely different. The funeral is very confusing and disorganized, even chaotic. There are people gathered in two different places for the service, and at one point I'm standing in back of everyone as I offer some introductory words, and they have to turn around to see me. This takes place in what seems like

---

2. Presbyterian Church (U.S.A.), *Constitution of the Presbyterian Church (U.S.A.)* (2007–2009), II: G-4.0101–G-4.0102. These sentences are not included in the most recent constitution of the Presbyterian Church (U.S.A.), as the constitution was simplified after 2009. Nonetheless, this excerpt from the 2007–2009 constitution captures my idea of the meaning of *church*.

an outdoor chapel set in a courtyard, but the pews are wooden and painted yellow. At another point I'm standing on a ladder—indeed, on the very top of the ladder—putting my hands into some soft bristle-like stuff on the ceiling of an area that is adjacent to the courtyard chapel. I have to put my hands up there to steady myself on the ladder, and people say cautionary things to me as I do this. My fingers sink into this soft stuff, which is colored orange or peach and feels like a deep carpet. I notice that there are two rooms where the service and other activities, perhaps the reception, will take place.

This dream came to me just weeks after the English-speaking congregation I was serving had merged with the Spanish-speaking congregation that had been worshipping separately in the same building for the past twelve years. I worked this dream with the dream group in my church, whose members had also experienced this merging process. I associated the two places in the dream with the two groups in our one newly merged congregation. The colors of the bristle-like material on the ceiling in the dream were the same as the colors recently used to paint the exterior of the church-owned house next door to the church. There had been some controversy within the congregation about the colors chosen to paint the house. The group helped me identify all these associations, and they also pointed out how I was supported by those around me in the church, portrayed in the dream by the people holding the ladder steady for me. This dream, according to the interpretation that I and the dream group developed together, was an accurate portrayal of my emotional state in my position as pastor of that church at the time of the dream. Though this dream was very specific to me and my position in the church at that time, it illustrates the way dreams help us see what is around us.

This example illustrates how dreams and dream work can inspire the life and work of a local congregation. In a larger context, I believe that dreams and dreaming may well have played a role in the founding of religion. Jeremy Taylor notes that the sacred texts of all the major faith traditions profess the central importance of dreams as a way of communicating directly with the divine.[3] He also makes a connection between dreams and the origin of religion, noting, "Most religions grew out of dream experiences of visitation by the dead."[4]

3. Taylor, *Where People Fly*, 114.
4. Taylor, "Dreams, Myths, and Social Justice."

All the religious traditions have developed their own attitudes toward dreams, often built upon the cultural context of their time and place. These views of dreaming have ranged from the acceptance and incorporation of dreams into religious life to their absolute rejection. The connection between religion and dreams is deeply buried and thus difficult to discover in the Judeo-Christian tradition. The Christian Bible does, however, contain several significant dream stories that I will cover in chapters 5 and 6, along with other significant dreams from the history of Christianity.

My own tradition is Judeo-Christian, specifically the Protestant faith that arose during the Reformation in sixteenth-century Europe. One of the legacies of the Protestant Reformation is a deep respect for scholarship and rationalism. This rationalism has led to the application of scientific tools to the study of faith and theology and to continued work to reconcile the Christian faith with the discoveries and insights of the scientific method. Tending to dreams in the Reformed tradition requires the use of three filters that are used to help measure the importance of a particular dream. These filters are history, tradition, and Scripture, and they will be covered in more detail later. Briefly, applying these filters means taking one's personal history, one's religious tradition, and one's personal understanding of Scripture into consideration when working to better understand a dream. This is a guiding principle behind this book and is the style of dream work that I recommend.

The Reformed tradition includes two elements that I want to focus on here. The first is the concept of the priesthood of all believers. Put simply, this means that each of us can be a mediator between God and each other. We do not need to rely on a person who has been set aside to be that mediator, as had been the role of the priest in the older church tradition. This concept was a core aspect of the sixteenth-century protest against the Roman Catholic system of the priest being the only one who could hear confession and grant absolution, as well as celebrate the Mass. The Protestant Reformers felt that if the Church returned to the New Testament model, believers could mediate God's grace to each other. In the Presbyterian Church (U.S.A.), for example, authority is vested in groups, such as elders, not in individuals. I consider a dream group to be a mediating body between God and the group members in the process of tending to individuals' dreams. This is an extension of the concept of the priesthood of all believers. As the Reformers saw themselves returning God's grace to the people in the pews, so the method of dream work that I advocate takes dream work away from the "experts" and returns it to the "common folks."

This method of dream work, known as Group Projective Dream Work, will be more fully explained in chapter 9. But its connection with church history is deeply rooted in the concept of the priesthood of all believers. The Protestant Reformers felt churches would be more faithfully and justly governed by groups than by individuals; similarly, dreams are better understood and paid attention to by groups than by individuals. Each of us will be wiser with the help of a group. Our dreams will be more richly explored with the help of others than by ourselves alone.

The second element of the Protestant Reformation relevant to dream work is the importance given to translating the Scripture into the vernacular languages of the people, thus enabling people to understand the Bible and the context of the biblical stories more fully. This parallels the need to learn the language of dreams. If we believe that we are meant to understand our dreams, we may find comfort and security in tending to our own dreams and the dreams of others. The language of dreams is universal because most dreams come to us as images and pictures rather than as words in our own language. Realizing that the images in our dreams are not wild or bizarre or even unique to us can give us a sense of freedom in looking at our dreams. This freedom can help us begin to pay attention to our dreams and get started on the adventure of living with our dreams. The parallel drawn here between reading the Bible in the vernacular and understanding the language of dreams as universal is not exact, but the ideas of seeking a better understanding of dreams and more universal access to the sacred texts of the Bible are related. The language that dreams speak is accessible to anyone who makes the effort to learn it (see chapter 4).

Resistance to Working with Dreams

Although dreams play a role in the Bible, the Bible reflects the tension between an unquestioning acceptance of dreams and the need to make sure that particular dreams have come from God. Some of this tension is also found in contemporary churches. The Christian church today faces many pressures from society at large, and Christian believers may look elsewhere than to the church for spiritual help. Church leaders discourage any use of dreams that might draw people away from their faith. They may speak negatively about dream work, but their real concern has to do with the misuse of dreams, not the dreams themselves. This position is not unique to Christians. Jewish author Shaul Bar agrees: "The Book of Deuteronomy does not necessarily repudiate the phenomenon of dreams. What it does reject are false prophets who use dreams for propaganda purposes and divert the people from the correct path."[5] Bar goes on to point out that one of the concerns about the use of dreams is determinism. He says, "The objection to dreams may be rooted in Israelite prophecy's rejection of determinism. . . . [The objection is based on] the view that everything that is going to happen has been preordained and that everything is known in advance."[6] Prophecy therefore allows people to repent and change their behavior, thus avoiding the prophesied fate. One of the advantages in doing dream work is indeed the possibility of finding alternative futures, alternative solutions to challenges, etc., which is the opposite of determinism.

Some people of faith object to the practice of incubating a dream. Incubating a dream means performing certain rituals and acts to encourage the appearance of a dream. This was a customary practice of the ancient Greeks. The position of the Hebrew Bible, and of the Christian tradition as well, is that dreams that are initiated by God are acceptable but that human efforts to initiate a dream should be discouraged.[7] Incubation, however, is different from simply asking God for help through one's dreams.[8] Incubation is not an attempt to manipulate God but rather to put oneself in the position to receive what God may offer. A variation on the ancient practice of incubation is to do a ritual or act to help one remember what one has dreamt.

There are other reasons for resistance to the use of dreams in the contemporary church. Frieda Fordham, for example, writes:

> To ancient man the dream was sent by God, and while the Church
> still allows this possibility (only very cautiously, and reserving to

5. Bar, *A Letter That Has Not Been Read*, 124.

6. Ibid. 141.

7. Bulkeley writes, "The basic theological argument against dream incubation seems to be this: The Judeo-Christian God, as a transcendent, omnipotent deity, cannot be beckoned by humans who simply perform a few ritual procedures and sleep in a temple. It is God who initiates contact with humans, not vice versa; the devil is more likely to heed such calls than is the Lord. Thus any human effort to evoke a dream revelation from God is impious and worthy of condemnation." He continues, in reference to the dream theophanies of Abram and Jacob, "In both cases the initiative for the dream revelation clearly lies with God; Abram and Jacob do not expect God to appear in their dreams." Bulkeley, *Spiritual Dreaming*, 128, 229n18.

8. See chapter 5 for a discussion of 1 Kgs 3:3–15, in which Solomon appears to have incubated a dream.

itself the right to adjudicate in the matter), popular opinion today has deprecated this kind of psychic activity to such an extent that it is often believed that dreams are merely the result of physical causes, such as sleeping in an uncomfortable position, or eating a heavy meal before going to bed.[9]

Over the past 150 years, the Christian church has responded both positively and negatively to the principles and practices of psychology. Freud was clearly against religion, and some churches extended their negative reaction to Freud to all psychologists and the field of psychology. Carl Jung encountered resistance from some Christians in relation to his work with dreams. Jung tried to clarify the argument by stating: "I am always coming up against the misunderstanding that a psychological treatment or explanation reduces God to 'nothing but' psychology. It is not a question of God at all, but of man's ideas of God, as I have repeatedly emphasized."[10]

Coming from a slightly different angle, Jeremy Taylor points out the irony in the way religions sometimes treat dreams.

> It is interesting to note in this connection that the sacred texts of the world's major religions (and the minor ones too, for that matter) all proclaim the central importance of dreams and dreaming as a means of direct communication with the Divine. However, at the same time, the vast majority of those religions also frown on, or even forbid, actual attention to dreams in their contemporary practice.[11]

How Dreams Can Help the Church

The premise of this book is that dreams can be helpful in the Christian church and in the faith lives of individual believers. Psychology, anthropology, philosophy, and the arts all benefit from looking at dreams, so why not the church as well? I believe strongly that dreams provide readily available access to the world of spirit, specifically through the work of the Holy Spirit, the third person of the Christian Trinity. In the life of the church, it is time to incorporate psychological knowledge into the spirituality of the church. This has already been happening in a variety of ways, but the

9. Fordham, *An Introduction to Jung's Psychology*, 102.

10. Jung, *Collected Works: Psychology and Religion; West and East*, 11:163.

11. Taylor, *Where People Fly*, 114.

use of dreams in the church has not been as well integrated as other psychological ideas have, such as family systems theory or various counseling and psychological inventory methods that are rooted in the field of psychology. A mystique of sorts has built up around dreams, and thus dreams have largely stayed in therapists' offices and not been allowed to "attend church."[12] Dreams and dream work, though, belong in the church. The use of psychological therapy by Christians is a good sign of openness to healing from sources outside the church. But what I'm arguing is that material that was once primarily used in the therapist's office should now be used by laypeople in general.

Carl Jung died in 1961, yet some of what he had to say about the Protestant church in Europe seems just as relevant to contemporary American mainline churches as it was over forty years ago to European churches. For example, "We have come to a serious pass. The exodus from the German Protestant Church is only one of many symptoms which should make it plain to the clergy that mere admonitions to believe, or to perform acts of charity, do not give modern man what he is looking for."[13]

Mainline American churches are today experiencing an exodus similar to the one several decades earlier that Jung was referring to. My understanding of what modern men and women are looking for is this: We are looking for a sense of the presence of God with us or in us. Dreams are readily available to us and offer us one way to find that presence of God in each of us. Dreams are not God, but they usher us into the realm of spirit where God's Holy Spirit reigns supreme.

What Is the Soul?

One of the ways that dreams and dream work can help the church is in recapturing the sense of soul. My favorite material on the soul is in the book *A Hidden Wholeness* by Parker Palmer. Palmer goes into considerable detail about his concept of the human soul. Below, I quote a passage that captures

12. Montague Ullman puts it this way: "While a certain amount of caution and responsibility is understandable in undertaking dream work, an overemphasis on the danger of dream work plays into the mystique that serious and effective dream work should be limited to the domain of the experts. This is a mystique that is gradually being put to rest as public awareness of and sophistication about dreams increases. Dream work belongs both in and beyond the consulting room." Ullman, introduction to Ullman and Limmer, *The Variety of Dream Experience*, viii.

13. Jung, *Collected Works: Psychology and Religion; West and East*, 11:333.

Palmer's thoughts on this topic as they relate to my understanding of the role that dreams can play in our lives.

> "Nobody knows what the soul is," says the poet Mary Oliver; "it comes and goes / like the wind over the water." But just as we can name the functions of the wind, so we can name some of the functions of the soul without presuming to penetrate its mystery:
>
> - The soul wants to keep us rooted in the ground of our own being, resisting the tendency of other faculties, like the intellect and ego, to uproot us from who we are.
>
> - The soul wants to keep us connected to the community in which we find life, for it understands that relationships are necessary if we are to thrive.
>
> - The soul wants to tell us the truth about ourselves, our world, and the relation between the two, whether that truth is easy or hard to hear.
>
> - The soul wants to give us life and wants us to pass that gift along, to become life-givers in a world that deals too much death.
>
> All of us arrive on earth with souls in perfect form. But from the moment of birth onward, the soul or true self is assailed by deforming forces from without and within: by racism, sexism, economic injustice, and other social cancers; by jealousy, resentment, self-doubt, fear, and other demons of the inner life.[14]

My view is that we encounter our soul when we dream, and working with our dreams is an attempt to grow soulfully. The soul is the territory that the Christian church has claimed responsibility for in human society. My favorite comment on the soul by Palmer is this:

> Like a wild animal, the soul is tough, resilient, resourceful, savvy, and self-sufficient: it knows how to survive in hard places. . . . Yet despite its toughness, the soul is also shy. Just like a wild animal, it seeks safety in the dense underbrush, especially when other people are around.[15]

---

14. Ibid., 32–34. Palmer quotes here from Mary Oliver's poem "Maybe" from *The Soul Is Here for Its Own Joy: Sacred Poems from Many Cultures* (Hopewell, NJ: Ecco Press, 1995).

15. Ibid., 58.

I don't know whether Palmer's discussion of the soul was influenced by other thinkers, but writers on dreams and dream work have addressed the soul in similar terms. According to Jung, for example:

> Often one has the impression that the personal psyche is running around this central point [of the dream or other symbol being considered] like a shy animal, at once fascinated and frightened, always in flight, and yet steadily drawing nearer.[16]

Jung's phrase "steadily drawing nearer" reminds me of the tendency of dreams, of recurring dreams in particular, to seek repeatedly to communicate with us until we get the message. Also, the phenomenon of our dream recall increasing the more we pay attention to our dreams may be analogous to Jung's idea that the soul wants to communicate, wants to be known.

Jungian Edward F. Edinger makes a similar statement about the wildness of living symbols. In reference to the symbol of the blood of Christ, he says:

> But the empirical method of analytical psychology requires that we attempt to strip away the protective, traditional context in order to examine the living symbol itself and to explore its spontaneous function in the individual psyche. It is as if we are visiting powerful wild animals in their natural habitat rather than looking at them confined to cages in a zoo.[17]

Edinger makes the connection between symbol and soul language (the latter phrase is my term, not his). This sense of visiting wild animals is what I believe takes place in the realm of dreams. Researcher Robert L. Van de Castle makes the connection between dreams and our belief in the soul:

> If our beliefs about the existence of a soul originated in dreams, then dreams should be recognized as having contributed a fundamental promise about the nature of human existence that has been a subject of debate and reflection in all civilizations and all ages.[18]

The realm of the soul has traditionally been the territory in which the church has had the most power and authority. I believe that churches that have moved away from working with the human soul have lost some of their power and authority. Working with dreams in a church setting is

16. Jung, *Dreams*, 292.
17. Edinger, *Ego and Archetype*, 225.
18. Van de Castle, *Our Dreaming Mind*, 42.

one way to get that power back and to begin to base the church's authority once again upon the realm of the soul, something that the church has a long tradition of dealing with.

The Church as a Container

I'm outside on the street I live on. A few of my neighbors are standing in the street having a discussion about how monks get rich. I explain to them that this does not happen, at least among Christian monks, because they all pool their money and live communally.

This dream was based on no particular day residue or stimulus in my waking life, but it reflects the somewhat defensive attitude that I have sometimes when talking with people who don't attend church about activities within the church. In the dream I clearly have one perspective on the church while my dream neighbors have another. The dream also played with me as I've occasionally entertained fantasies of becoming a monk.

I believe many dreamers can be helped by the container that the church provides. By *container* I mean the conceptual framework within which we function. The Christian church provided the ethical and conceptual framework for much of Western civilization for many centuries. That level of influence has receded more into the background in our own time, but the church with its doctrines, ethics, and wealth of stories can be a great help to people of faith working with their dreams. Though the organized or institutionalized church has drawbacks, the positive elements of the historical, organized Christian church provide a good backdrop for groups desiring to do dream work. Over the two thousand years of its existence, the Christian church has seen a variety of different spiritualities and practices, and its winnowing of these practices has helped believers learn from those who have gone before them. For those open to the tradition of the church, there is much to learn from the history of Christian spirituality and practice. As we work with our dreams and wonder about what kind of attitude to have towards them or what kinds of follow-up actions we should take, our reliance upon the historical Christian church can provide boundaries around our work, a container within which we can function.

Because the church as a whole has not paid much attention to dreams, people wind up looking elsewhere for help with their dreams. This is a sad loss, both for the dreamers and for the church. As mentioned in the opening of this chapter, the Judeo-Christian experience with dreams goes back nearly four thousand years. Throughout most of that time, the church was reliably able to deal with the material in dreams based on faith rooted in experience, checked by the practice of self-reflection and self-criticism.[19]

One of the dangers of dream work is that we can become so focused upon our self and our dreams that we become enclosed in a world composed of only our self and our self-focused images. The church can help prevent dreamers from becoming so self-centered. Christian discipleship encourages us to focus not only on our own spiritual growth but also on the good of other people. Christian faith is outward—it is other-directed. Self-fulfillment when those around us are suffering is not the response that Jesus Christ calls us to. The human tendency toward narcissism is something that needs to be held in rein. My belief is that the more we understand ourselves, the better we are able to relate to others and reach out to others, and working with our dreams is one way to improve our self-understanding.[20] In other words, dream work within the church encourages dreamers to be more outwardly directed.

The way the church passes on the faith to believers provides another area of support or containment for our dream life. The life of most churches is composed of worship, Bible study, fellowship, and service, and all these aspects of church life are helpful for spiritual growth. These can also be viewed as complementary activities to the introspection involved in doing dream work.

In addition to the support that the local congregation can provide, the larger institutional church can also provide various forms of support. The benefits of belonging to an organized religion are many. Garret Keizer writes of "standing on the shoulders of giants," referring to the ongoing influence of the great theologians and leaders who have kept the church

19. According to Meier and Wise, "Old Testament and New Testament heroes and the early Christians knew dreams were helpful in leading them to the center of spiritual reality. We are on the same path. Far from New Age, we are recovering the ancient footprints of the saints." Meier and Wise, *Windows of the Soul*, 144.

20. Calvin S. Hall and Vernon J. Nordby write: "Jung counsels that less emphasis should be placed on obtaining total self-realization, and more emphasis should be placed on knowledge of one's self. Self-knowledge is the path to self-realization. This is an important distinction, because many people want to fulfill themselves without having the slightest knowledge of themselves. They want instant perfection, a miracle that will transform them into a fully realized person. Actually, the task is the most arduous one [we face] in [our lives], requiring constant discipline, persistent efforts, and the highest responsibility and wisdom." Hall and Nordby, *A Primer of Jungian Psychology*, 52.

faithful throughout the ages.[21] We benefit from the insights and experiences of those who have gone before us in the life of faith. As a practitioner among the Reformed family of Christians, I benefit from the thinking and writings of Martin Luther, John Calvin, Francis de Sales, Karl Rahner, and many others in regards to the Christian faith. These are giants who help me see farther and more clearly understand certain issues of faith. Luther and Calvin, in particular, have made contributions to today's thinking about dreams (see chapter 6).

The institutional church also helps us avoid mistakes and move beyond the church's historical self-centeredness. In its two thousand years of existence, the Christian church has explored ideas and ways of life that work as well as many that do not. Thus, we do not have to reinvent the wheel, nor do we have to repeat the mistakes of those who have gone before us. In the area of dreams and dream work, we can learn from the people of the past who have used their dreams to veer away from the main life of the church to their detriment.

Organized religion does have negative aspects, characteristics shared by nearly every organized religion that I'm aware of. These are the tendency towards existing for themselves, becoming fascinated and obsessed by power, and turning away from and discouraging the very types of insights and creative energies that inspired the religion in the first place. There is no denying these qualities of institutionalized religion, and most practitioners will recognize these tendencies. But that is not the full story, as most practitioners will agree.

One last way that dream work can help the church is a form of evangelism. Dreamers who are members of local churches sometimes have the opportunity to talk about their dreams and dream groups with strangers. For example, a member of a church-based dream group may invite someone at the grocery store or bank or dentist's office who expresses an interest in dreams to attend their dream group. This kind of outreach has resulted in people who aren't involved in organized religion attending dream groups held in churches. One of the ways small groups work in the church is to shepherd people into the church through the church's small groups. Dream groups function in this way, as do many other kinds of small groups.

Many people have been hurt by the church through the unhealthy behavior of church members or the perpetuation of unhealthy ideas about the Bible or church doctrine. Some of these people may have found other

21. Keizer, "Reasons to Join," 29.

means of making sense out of their life that are separate from organized religion. But for others, the most helpful experience might be to have their church-inflicted wounds healed within the church itself. An analogy to this would be an estranged family member having an experience of powerful healing by reconciling with family members. Dream groups can play a role in this kind of spiritual healing. If dream groups that are related to churches or have church members participating in them reach out to wounded believers, a great service can be rendered. The newcomer may end up associating with a local church through an avenue they might never otherwise have considered.

The kind of healing referred to above should not be confused with a deeper need for healing that might require psychotherapy. The practice of dream work I advocate is not to be used as a substitute for therapy with a professional therapist. Therapy practiced by trained professionals is focused on the healing of patients who may be so deeply wounded they are not able to function in their daily lives. My practice of dream work is influenced by my training in spiritual direction, which is focused on spiritual growth. Spiritual growth and healing are not necessarily separate. All of us have various wounds that need healing, and all of us can grow in our spiritual life. But the boundary between the type of dream work I practice, Group Projective Dream Work, and therapeutic dream work is a matter of the level of health and ability to function of the dreamer.[22] All of us dream and all of us can make use of our dreams. Our dreams can give us insight into the deeper workings of our life. For practicing Christians, the better we understand our inner workings, the better disciples we will be. Some of us may have been deeply wounded at various times in life, and sometimes therapy may be needed before we can be a disciple at all. A good dream group leader or pastor will know when to refer a dreamer to therapy. But for the majority of people, dream work can make their discipleship all the more effective.

My interest in dream work is as a pastor and Christian leader, not as a therapist. I believe the mainline Christian churches in America need a deeper connection to our ancient roots, our soul. Thus, this is another reason dream work belongs in the church. The movement toward a deeper spirituality in the mainline churches in America can benefit from the use of dreams as spiritual tools. One benefit of deeper spirituality, and of dream

22. On this topic, Jeremy Taylor writes, "That's one of the reasons I do this work as a minister rather than a therapist. I'm really interested in the people who are not driven by neurosis so much as they are by a longing for greater awareness of the Divine." Quoted in Gardenhire and Ludwig. "Dreams, Communing with the Divine," 8.

work in particular, is the opening up of the imagination. With greater imagination, new forms and ways of "being church" can be developed. According to Ben Johnson, "To foster new life, stagnant congregations must embrace the reality of their present context and imagine their life in new form."[23] Wherever the need for imagination is brought up, I see the value of tending to dreams. Dreams are great vehicles of creativity and imagination.

Dreams provide us with very real, very present experiences of the Spirit of God at work in our lives and the world around us. Paying attention to our experiences of God is something the church does well, when it is living at its best. Working with our dreams can have positive effects on the ways in which we pray and sense answers to our prayers and the ways we receive guidance, as well as on our sense of spiritual accompaniment. These are experiences in the life of faith that Christians have shared down through the ages, and the sharing of these experiences can be nurtured within the organized church.

Dream work is not the salvation of the church, but dreams are easily accessible to all, and dream work should be one of the tools we use to help revitalize the church, to re-introduce the modern church to the realm of spirit, the work of the soul. Dream work references past traditions of Christian history, traditions that can be of great use today. Dreams can provide the energy, the imagination, and the creativity that is much needed in contemporary mainline Christian churches in the United States. As we wrestle with the changing demographics in our neighborhoods and the changing technologies in our society and seek to be faithful in all places, dreams can be of great help to us. Likewise, the church can contribute to the current understanding of dreams and to the practice of dream work through the application some of its traditions to dream work.

23. The title of Johnson's book from which this is taken, 95 Theses for the Church, is a play on Martin Luther's 95 Theses of 1517 that symbolize the beginning of the Protestant Reformation. In another of Johnson's theses he notes, "Most congregations need transformation and revitalization which includes:

A Recovery of a Sense of the Presence of God,
A Shift from 'Maintenance' to Mission,
The Revitalization of Worship,
The Liberation of the Laity,
The Selection and Nurturing of Mentors,
The Formation of Small, Intentional Groups.

Four of these six tools for transformation (1, 3, 5, and 6) are addressed by the formation of dream groups. Johnson, 95 Theses for the Church, 27, 36.

3

Small Groups in the Church

The story is told in *The Thousand and One Nights* of a merchant from Baghdad who squandered his fortune and was reduced to a life of misery and destitution. One night the merchant had a dream in which a man appeared and said, "Your fortune lies in Cairo. Go and see it there." The merchant awoke and, deciding he had nothing to lose, traveled to Cairo. But as the Almighty would have it, when the poor merchant arrived in Cairo he was mistaken for a thief and thrown into prison, where he was mercilessly beaten. Three days later the chief of police questioned the merchant. When asked why he had come to Cairo, the merchant described his dream. The chief of police burst out laughing and said, "You fool, I too have heard a voice in my sleep, not just once but on three occasions. It said: 'Go to Baghdad, and in a cobbled street lined with palm trees you will find such-and-such a house, with a courtyard of grey marble; under the white marble fountain a great sum of money is buried.' But would I go? Of course not. Yet, fool that you are, you have come all the way to Cairo on the strength of one idle dream." The chief of police finally took pity on the gullible merchant and released him. The merchant expressed his humble thanks and hurried back to Baghdad—for the chief's dream had described the merchant's own house, and when he dug under the fountain in his courtyard the merchant uncovered great treasure.[1]

I n relating this story of the Baghdad merchant, Kelly Bulkeley notes: "If we listen carefully to the dreams of *other people* we may be surprised by the valuable treasures we find."[2] I'm familiar with several versions of this story, and they all remind me of the story of Joseph and his family in

1. For the complete story, see Bulkeley, *Spiritual Dreaming*, 1.

2. Ibid., italics in original.

Genesis 37–50 and of the way dreams, when we pay attention to them, give blessings in unexpected ways.

The story of the Baghdad merchant makes a strong argument for listening to the dreams of others and, if appropriate, acting upon them. This highlights the value of dream groups, where the participants spend much time listening to the dreams of other people. There are other settings besides groups for working with dreams, such as on one's own or in the contexts of therapy and spiritual direction. This chapter will cover three important aspects of tending to one's dreams in a group setting: the historical roots of small groups in the church, ground rules and issues related to safety in groups, and the contemporary dream movement.

A Brief History of Small Groups in the Church

The increased popularity of small groups in American churches in the last generation or so is not something particularly new. Small groups do meet the need for community in our individualistic society, where we feel increasingly isolated from each other. Churches in our day have made use of small groups to meet congregants' needs for companionship and community. But companionship and small groups have actually been a practice of the Christian church since its inception. The modern American small group movement within the church is simply an example of a past tradition that has been recovered and put to modern use. In like manner, the contemporary growth of spiritual direction in Protestant denominations meets the need for companions on the journey of faith (see chapter 7 for more examples of ancient practices revived for use in the modern church).

The early Christian church began in small groups known as house churches. These were groups that met together in members' homes for worship, support, and fellowship.[3] In the first thousand years of the church's existence, communities also formed around hermits who were holy men and women, who became known for their wisdom. These gatherings were eventually organized into monasteries. One of the more well-known examples of the use of small groups in more recent Christian church history is the Methodist movement in America and England in the first part of the 1700s. John Wesley was influenced by the small group practices of German Moravians he met on his cross-Atlantic journey and adapted some of their practices into gatherings that were called "bands" or "classes." These small

3. See Acts 2:43–47 and 4:32–37.

groups were pivotal to the explosive growth of Methodism in both England and North America.[4]

Small groups have thus long offered support, education, and worship to Christians, helping the church form its followers into better disciples. In the current setting of mainline churches, the need for spiritual formation is again growing, and churches and leaders are seeking either new forms of spiritual practices or traditional practices that can be profitably revived. Small groups provide a time-tested option for the church.[5] Doing dream work in small groups is one variation among many others of this historical practice. Although dreams were used in churches in the past, as described in chapter 6, that practice has fallen out of use in most mainline churches. I hope this book will encourage the reintroduction of dreams and dream work into the small group work of local churches.

Ground Rules for Groups

> Paul [sharing his dream]: I dream I'm working on a landscaping project, but I can't get the water to flow the way I want it to. I keep going back and forth adjusting some of the irrigation pieces to get the water to flow right.
>
> Paul's wife: I'll tell you what that dream means. I'm tired of you continuing to work when you could be retired and spending more time traveling with me. If you don't change your ways soon, you are going to be in trouble. I'm going away this weekend by myself!

This interchange between Paul and his wife is a dramatic example of abuse of a dream group. Paul's wife used this opportunity to say something to him that she had not felt she could say in any other place or way. She could have made a connection between the dream contents and the issues in their marriage, but that is not what happened, and I, as the dream group leader, was unprepared for the challenge when this exchange came up. This experience taught me that there is a clear need for strong ground rules in dream groups. As it turned out, Paul's wife did take her trip by herself the

---

4. Watson, "Methodist Spirituality," in *Exploring Christian Spirituality*, 179–82.

5. Ben Johnson mentions small groups in two of his 95 theses. Number 57 states, "The best way to initiate the needed transformations in the church will be through the formation of small intentional groups—cadres of apostolic believers," and number 59 is, "Persons called to this adventure must agree to meet together regularly for an agreed upon length of time in an agreed upon place." Johnson, *95 Theses for the Church*, 55–57.

next weekend, and by the following month their marriage seemed to have returned to business as usual, with Paul still working more than his wife felt he should. But their marriage held together and life went on, as did that particular dream group.

When I first looked into the International Association of the Study of Dreams (IASD) I was struck by the group's clearly worded ethical statement (see appendix E). People who are interested in their dreams have to look hard for help working with their dreams because of the lack of acceptance of dream work and of the relatively low perceived value of dreams within general society and also within the church. Not everyone who works with dreams, however, does so from a position of responsibility, integrity, and accountability. The fact that the IASD developed an ethical statement in its early days is evidence of the need for such guidelines.

People come to dream groups for a variety of reasons, and it is important to set ground rules that will respect the experience of the dreamer and of everyone else in the group, including the leader. The safety of those inquiring into their dreams is of primary concern among all reputable dream workers and researchers.[6] Dream group members' emotions, sense of self, soul, etc., all need to be kept safe. A sense of trust and confidentiality must be built up in a dream group.[7] Suggestions for dream group process and etiquette will be covered in chapter 9.

I find two concepts very helpful in regards to this issue of safety in dream groups: the clearness committee and the circle of trust, both explored in depth in the writings of Parker Palmer.[8] Some of the principles contained

6. As Montague Ullman states, "Questions of safety do arise. Any process, regardless of how intrinsically safe it may be, can be misused. It seems to me that the rewards gained by educating the public to the significance of dreams and the way to work with them in a supportive social context far exceed the risk involved." Ullman, introduction to *The Variety of Dream Experience*, xii.

7. Jeremy Taylor emphasizes the need for confidentiality in dream groups: "In order to proceed with this risk taking and self-revelation, a sense of relative safety and security is absolutely necessary. At a minimum, dream group participants need to feel relatively secure in the knowledge that they are not going to unexpectedly meet the intimate details they have shared about their lives and feelings around the next corner in the form of gossip." Taylor, *The Living Labyrinth*, 1.

8. I've adapted Palmer's definition, in which he applies the clearness committee to a couple discerning marriage. Here are his words: "A small group of meeting members gathers with the couple several times to pray, to ask caring but probing questions, to explore issues the couple might not have considered on their own, to listen carefully to how the couple answers—and to let the couple listen anew to themselves." Palmer, "The Clearness Committee," 37.

in these concepts could be adapted for any kind of group gathering in any social setting, but the focus here is on their application to dream groups.

The clearness committee is a Quaker process used to help a "focus person" discern the next step in a particular situation. In a clearness committee, a small group gathers to pray, to ask caring but probing questions, to explore issues, and to let the focus person listen anew to themselves.[9] The respect for the focus person (in dream groups, this is the person sharing their dream) and the "space" given them are the great gifts of the clearness committee.[10] I've experienced feelings of discomfort in dream groups when a group member tries to "interpret" the dreams of other members and does not use the agreed-upon formula for dream group etiquette in making their comments. In one group, a member often paid too much attention to the clock in such a way as to run roughshod over the emotions of the person sharing a dream. Paying attention to the time is an important role for the group leader, but it is sometimes done insensitively. Such behavior does not allow for the best conditions of safety in a small group.

What strikes me the most in the clearness committee process is the sense of respect for the person who is the focus of the event. Utmost care is given to listening to the focus person. Any questions are meant to help the person clarify his or her thinking. This is the opposite of what often happens in ordinary human communications, when a question is actually a veiled statement or a question begs the answer the questioner believes to be the truth. The general guidelines for a clearness committee address guarding the emotional safety of the group members, showing respect for the dreamer, doing more listening than speaking, and asking no "leading questions" (questions aimed at an answer the questioner wants to hear); these all make for good boundaries in a dream group.

The idea of the "circle of trust" developed by Parker Palmer is a very similar concept to the clearness committee. The circle of trust is "a community that knows how to welcome the soul and help us hear its voice."[11] Palmer makes a distinction between a circle of trust and what he calls "T groups," or encounter groups, which were popular in the 1960s and 1970s

9. Palmer offers a humorous quip about the origin of the term *clearness committee*: "It sounds like a name from the '60s, and it is—the 1660s!" Palmer, *A Hidden Wholeness*, 134.

10. Palmer adds, "The function of the clearness committee is not to give advice or alter and 'fix' people but to help people remove obstacles and discover the divine assistance that is within." Ibid., 38.

11. Ibid., 22.

among people who were looking for personal growth and change. He says: "T groups, even at their best, do not welcome the soul, which distrusts confrontation because its dynamics run so much deeper than momentary feelings."[12] He also offers the following reasons why we need others to help us welcome the soul:

- The inner journey is too taxing to be made solo. Without support we become weary or fearful, and are likely to quit.

- The path is too deeply hidden to be traveled without company.

- We need the courage a community can provide.[13]

Each one of these points that Palmer makes for circles of trust can be used verbatim to describe dream groups. They provide the framework and boundaries that a dream group can use to ensure the safety of the participants and the boundaries within which the group should operate.

The Modern Dream Work Movement

Over the past one hundred years, working with dreams has grown in popularity, largely due to the rise of modern psychology. In the last few decades, a movement has developed to take dreams out of analysts' offices into living rooms and meeting rooms, wherever people gather. As one of the founders of this movement says:

> The "grass roots" dream movement in the United States is a remarkable phenomenon, countering psychoanalytic dogma that a trained analyst is needed to help people "decode" the "hidden" meaning of their dreams, a meaning that dreamers "defend" themselves from comprehending. In contrast, the current crop of dream facilitators takes the position that dreams reveal more than they conceal and that the communal sharing of dream reports can be edifying to all group members, even those who have not brought a dream to share.[14]

The previous chapter discussed the concept developed during the Protestant Reformation of the priesthood of all believers. Some of the same

---

12. Ibid., 23.
13. Ibid., 26.
14. Stanley Krippner, introduction to Lasley, *Honoring the Dream*, ix.

principles behind that concept are at work in the philosophy behind dream groups. According to Justina Lasley,

> When only one person looks at a dream there is only one viewpoint. Just as a diamond reflects its brilliance from each of its many facets, our understanding of a dream is enlightened when it is considered from a multitude of angles. The group helps the dreamer look at the dream from a variety of vantage points.[15]

A group can make a more thorough and reasoned decision than can an individual. Though committees may take longer in the decision process, the decisions made by committees tend to be more thoroughly thought through and to anticipate possible objections. Similarly, a dream discussed by a group will reveal more meaning than if just one person is hearing it.

There has been good work done on the ethics, parameters, and benefits of working with dreams in groups. Savary, Berne, and Williams, for example, outline the benefits of doing dream work in group settings. Note some parallels to the circles of trust discussed above.

- Learning to listen more actively;

- Learning to formulate questions;

- Learning to work together without taking over control of the group;

- Getting practice in analytic thinking, creative thinking, choicemaking, and intuition;

- Learning how to recognize and identify different kinds of energies;

- Learning to suggest tasks that respond to existing energies;

- Learning to tell stories;

- Learning how to get meaning out of symbols;

- Learning to confront people and challenge them;

- Learning to accept and affirm people.[16]

Kelly Bulkeley also describes the larger value of sharing dreams in groups:

> Dream sharing groups enable participants to gain valuable insights into the relations between their personal lives and the broader social world in which they live. Furthermore, many dream sharing groups give people a means of understanding *others*, of

15. Lasley, *Honoring the Dream*, 94.

16. Savary et al., *Dreams and Spiritual Growth*, 180.

recognizing their connections with people who are different from themselves.[17]

Benefits of Working Dreams with Others

I dream I'm standing in an urban area with a group of people, four of whom are family and friends. There is a series of old-fashioned billboards surrounding the area, with large incandescent light bulbs providing the illumination. Each billboard is in a different foreign language, some of which I recognize, like German or French, and others that are in a totally different character system, like maybe Arabic or Chinese. I'm looking at them with my four friends and family members and we are trying to figure out what they mean. My companions offer suggestions, but no one is sure. Although they all mean well in trying to help me figure out the meaning, I feel like no one is able to understand me or help me. The last billboard is full of Xs and Os. I wake wondering what it all means.

The woman who shared this dream had never done dream work in a group. She had tried to work on some of her dreams alone but did not feel she had had much success. This dream mystified her, so she brought it to a demonstration dream group, a group that gathered together one time only for the purpose of exploring the value of dreams in one's spiritual life. As she explained her background, she indicated that her husband had died suddenly at work one day, about four months earlier. The family and friends who were in the dream were those who had been trying hardest to provide comfort and support for her. Yet, she felt that they just did not understand what she was going through. As the group worked with the dream, they pointed out that the Xs and Os are a kind of universal language for hugs and kisses. With further work, the dreamer felt that these hugs and kisses represented support that her dream was telling her about, whether they were hugs and kisses from her departed husband, or from God, or from somewhere else. She felt great comfort from this understanding, which came to her from the group, not from her own efforts. This was a very clear and rather dramatic example of the value of a group in working with an individual on her dream.

I have experienced repeatedly that a group can provide "extra eyes and ears" for the dreamer as he or she tries to understand a particular dream.

17. Bulkeley, *Visions of the Night*, 35, italics in original.

Often a dreamer, after having shared a dream and listening to others' responses, will exclaim something like, "Wow, I never saw that in the dream." Then the group will respond, "That's what we are here for." Such moments illustrate to the whole group the value of working dreams in a group setting. When I myself have a dream that seems to have a great deal of power attached to it but I don't yet understand the dream, I tell myself, "This is a dream that I want to take to my dream group." That process has yet to fail me, and I come away from the group with an expanded and more helpful understanding of the dream.

Not everything that a group offers the dreamer will be helpful, and the dreamer always has the choice of accepting or rejecting the help offered. It may be the case, too, that the dreamer will make note of all comments at the time they are made and only later find that one of the comments turns out to be insightful after all, perhaps after the dreamer has done some further work on the dream after the original group meeting; for whatever reason, the dreamer is not at first able to hear or to accept what is said. It may be that only when the dreamer is in the emotional safety of being alone with the dream that the dreamer can find an association, an "aha" about the dream that he or she did not see when the group worked with the dream.

One way to understand this is to carefully apply the thinking behind Jesus' saying in Matt 7:5: "Take the log out of your own eye before you tell someone else about the speck in their own eye" (NRSV). Jesus is talking about our human tendency to be judgmental towards others without seeing ourselves honestly and clearly. Using a group to help us understand our dreams is a way to act on what Jesus is saying. We are usually blind to our own faults and shortcomings, but others can see us more clearly. So too with dream work; we have our own particular blinders on that keep us from seeing the wider picture of our life. These blinders work the same way in our dreams, and others can often see more clearly than we can. The precaution must always be added that group members should respect the dreamer's feelings and emotional boundaries. One of the ways to ensure this is to use Group Projective Dream Work, a specific method of working with dreams in groups (see chapter 9).

From the early days of the Christian church to the current dream work movement, the value of sharing dreams and seeking personal and spiritual growth is evident. I recommend doing dream work in a group setting for the reasons outlined in this chapter. Though we may not get rich from listening to the dreams of others, as did the merchant of Baghdad, there is great value in listening to our own and others' dreams. This can best be done in groups that follow generally accepted ethical guidelines and pay attention to maintaining the safety and level of trust that the human soul needs to reveal itself.

Taylor summarizes well the benefits of working on dreams with others: "Sharing and exploring dreams with other compatible people on some sort of regular basis is the single, best, most reliable, and most amusing way of reaching greater conscious understanding of the deeper layers of meaning and psychospiritual significance that are the foundation of our waking experience."[18]

The dream group that I began in my local parish ten years ago as part of my project for the Doctor of Ministry degree has continued to meet up to the present. In an evaluative survey taken after I retired from that parish, the group members listed the benefits of the group for them. These benefits included group intimacy and spiritual depth, emotional support for group members, a greater awareness of issues facing individuals or the parish, and a variety of other benefits.[19] This is strong evidence of the value of dream groups that meet in local churches.

18. Taylor, *The Living Labyrinth*, 1.

19. Nelson, "Benefits of a Parish Dream Group, 182–91.

4

The Content of Dreams

Tell all the truth but tell it slant—
Success in Circuit lies
Too bright for our infirm Delight
The Truth's superb surprise

—Emily Dickinson, "Tell All the Truth"

D reams speak in images, symbols, and metaphors. This may be because dreaming preceded human language; dreams originally needed to present themselves in some form other than words, and, for this, pictures do the job well.[1] One of the difficulties that beginners to dream work encounter is the question of how to interpret the images that dreams use to communicate with us. What do the pictures in our dreams mean? As stated on the back cover of Robert Hoss's book *Dream Language*, "Don't miss the message simply because you don't understand the language."[2] The question of how to understand the language of dreams is of great importance to dreamers who are serious about doing dream work. This chapter will look at theories about the images in dreams and then briefly focus on some specific images to enable you to become more comfortable working with your dream images.

Perhaps the most controversial theories about the images in dreams come from the great pioneer of the unconscious, Sigmund Freud. His preoccupation with sex makes his theories appealing in our current culture, but that approach cuts both ways. As Van de Castle says, "Through his

1. Taylor, Plenary Address.
2. Hoss, *Dream Language*.

intense focus upon the neurotic, infantile, and sexual aspects of dreams, Freud gave dreams a bad name."[3]

Freud may have sex appeal, but he doesn't have dream appeal! Meier and Wise offer one of the best analyses of this issue of the meaning of dream symbols, especially as it relates to the differences between the theories of Freud and Jung:

> The dream is not a puzzle to be solved as much as it is a mystery to be explored. Freud's theories erred by being too logical. . . . For example, if a person dreamed of a key opening a lock, Freud concluded the dream was about sexual intercourse. Jung discovered the opposite approach was needed. We must associate to the symbol. . . . [A lock and key illustration] might more accurately convey an opportunity to 'open up' a new relationship. Perhaps some new truth needed to be "unlocked." Maybe the dream is telling us that we hold in our hands "the key to the future." . . . . Each of these interpretations could be correct under the right circumstances. Only the context of the dream can tell us.[4]

Some other examples of symbols illustrate that assumptions about the universal meaning of particular symbols do not hold true. Apples, for example, have a variety of associations for most of us but would mean something different to a person who is allergic to them. Or, think of the value that cows have in the United States versus India. One of the major premises behind Group Projective Dream Work is that only the dreamer can say for sure which associations have the most power for him or her. This style of dream work allows the individual the most freedom, but it also allows for the universalism of symbols to be explored. I like Taylor's larger view, which is described well by Ann Faraday:

> All the great dream theories of the past contain valuable elements of truth, and so [Jeremy Taylor] urges us to look at every dream for a "Freudian" sexual meaning, an "Adlerian" struggle-for-identity meaning, a "Jungian" archetypal meaning, an "Edgar Cayce" physical-health meaning, an "existential" revelation of the dreamer's concerns with death, a "psychic" meaning for the future, and a religious meaning in terms of higher spiritual realities![5]

3. Van de Castle, *Our Dreaming Mind*, 139.

4. Meier and Wise, *Windows of the Soul*, 23.

5. Faraday, introduction to Taylor, *Dream Work*, 3.

One of the beauties of the human species is the uniqueness of each individual person. That same uniqueness plays in the world of our dreams and the images used by our dreams. In our search for universal symbols, we run the risk of overlooking the individuality and uniqueness of each person. Jung speaks to this:

> The sexual theory and the wish theory, like the power theory, are valuable points of view without, however, doing anything like justice to the profundity and richness of the human psyche. Had we a theory that did, we could then content ourselves with learning a method mechanically. It would then be simply a matter of reading certain signs that stood for fixed contents, and for this it would only be necessary to learn a few semiotic rules by heart. Knowledge and correct assessment of the conscious situation would then be as superfluous as in the performance of a lumbar puncture.[6]

Another of the difficulties with dream images is the contrast between the values we hold in our waking lives and the seeming ability of dreams to ignore and even contradict our waking values. This will be illustrated by some of the images discussed below. Because dreams are not "real," in that they are not necessarily reflective of our waking behavior, they can say things to us in ways that we may not be able or willing to hear otherwise. Bulkeley and Bulkley describe these "unmoral dreams" as follows:

> Indeed, transgressing traditional moral boundaries can be seen as the precondition for creativity and the resolution of seemingly impossible problems and conflicts. The creative power of dreaming derives in large part from the freedom we have while asleep to explore, in a safe and harmless environment, those areas of our cultural world where we feel most troubled and confused. The images and feelings that emerge have the beneficial effect of reorienting the dreamer's sense of selfhood, clarifying important truths and integrating previously alienated elements of identity.[7]

The concept of mistaken literalism[8] is helpful to understand as you work with your dreams. This is an important concept in dream work, and every dream worker needs to be familiar with the idea. Now I will move on to what I call "the gallery of images." This selection of dream images or themes is not exhaustive but is intended to give the reader some reference

---

6. Jung, *Dreams*, 46.

7. Bulkeley and Bulkley, *Dreaming Beyond Death*, 86.

8. See the discussion of mistaken literalism in chapter 9.

points to images and themes that show up in dreams. I will explore death, sex, the shadow, the anima/animus image, and the images often found in nightmares.

Death in Dreams

Dreams of death and murder are profound dreams of new life, as paradoxical as that seems. These kinds of dreams occur when someone is facing a deep change in their life, such as an adult going through a major life transition. The old self has to die in order for a new self to become a reality. Children may be prone to these kinds of nightmares for similar reasons.[9] As children experience transitions from one stage of life to another, their dreams may express the fear and anxiety they feel but cannot articulate. The rate of emotional growth in young children is much faster than in most adults. Going to school for the first time, changing schools, being home alone, getting a first job, learning to drive, dating, etc., are all experiences that require an increase in maturity, a greater amount of 'growing up.' There are many stages in the lives of children in which they metaphorically have to die to the younger child and be reborn into the more responsible child.

Those who are new to dream work or who are unsophisticated regarding their dreams may be frightened by their dreams of death. Part of this fear has to do with the concept of mistaken literalism mentioned above. Dream researchers, however, view these types of dreams more positively. Meier and Wise make the association with the Christian concept of resurrection: "Death dreams generally help us get ready for resurrection. Because they signal transformation, we can, in the most positive sense, call them visits from Doctor Death."[10] Nan Zimmerman has a more secular and psychological perspective: "In our dreams death wears many faces and looks on life from many angles. Most typically death dreams deal not with the loss of life but the loss of a way of life or change not yet fully absorbed."[11] Jeremy Taylor makes the following statement about death in dreams based on his rich experience with dreams and dream work:

> The image of death, when it appears in dreams, is the single most
> common and frequent archetypal metaphor of real growth and

9. See Bulkeley and Siegal, *Dreamcatching*. 59–91.

10. Meier and Wise, *Windows of the Soul*, 192.

11. Zimmerman, "After the Dream Is Over," in Ullman and Limmer, *The Variety of Dream Experience*, 34.

change in the dreamer's psyche. . . . 'Death' is the most common archetypal symbolic image of psychospiritual growth and change; and when that death is self-inflicted in a dream, it implies that this time, it's going to work. This time, the dreamer's conscious effort to reshape his or her psyche and personality to overcome the habits of [addictive behavior] is likely to succeed. Suicide becomes an exquisite metaphor of the personality that is still addicted choosing to transform itself so radically and fundamentally that the only appropriate metaphor is self-inflicted death.[12]

If we can get beyond mistaken literalism in interpreting our dreams, and if we can accept the changes and transformations in life gracefully, dreaming of death may indeed be a welcome experience. It means we are on the verge of being transformed into something new and better.

Sex in Dreams

I dream of being in a familiar house, maybe the neighborhood where I grew up. I am getting ready to go visit one of the neighbor girls and have sex with her.

Dreams of sex, particularly for those within the church, may violate the dreamer's waking-life moral code and be all the more difficult to work with as a result. Here, I'm speaking of the dreams of adults, not what are called the "wet dreams" of adolescent boys, which function as a necessary part of their physiological growth. If I should dream of sex with someone other than my wife, I may wake into a moral dilemma. My dream self seemed to have no such dilemma, so how do I make sense of this? In the same way that dreams of death tend to symbolize something else, so do dreams of sexual activity. Here are a couple of thought-provoking quotes on this topic. Robert A. Johnson comments, "Sex is the one symbol in dreams that is always creative. Even if it occurs in violent form in a dream, still, it is speaking to us of reconciliation and creation."[13] Johnson may be making a pun on the "procreative" aspects of sex. Meier and Wise, from a Christian perspective, pose questions that provide deeper insights into images of sex in dreams: "For sexual dreams, consider the Alter-Gender [anima/animus] issues. Who is this person, and how do we know him or her? What is the

---

12. Taylor, *The Living Labyrinth*, 56, 62.

13. Johnson, *Owning Your Own Shadow*, 116.

context of our relationship? What do we like about this person? Dislike? Does this person attract us? What characteristics do we see in him or her?"[14]

The issue of creativity that Johnson mentions in the first quote is an initial association that can easily be made. Sexuality is most closely associated with reproduction or procreation and only secondarily associated with pleasure and depth of relationship. The ancient traditional association with sex found in myth, legend, and primitive religions is that of fertility. The questions that Meier and Wise ask in the above quote can be very fruitful in working a dream that involves a sexual encounter, no matter who the dream character is. This was the direction I took with the dream I mention in the opening of this section, the dream of sex with a neighbor girl from my adolescence. So much time had elapsed between the dream and my childhood in that neighborhood that I could no longer recall any qualities in her that I might have wanted to appropriate. The way I worked with the dream that day was to see this dream character, the former neighbor girl, as a representation of the alter-gender energy in myself and in the situation in my life when I had that particular dream, an affirmation of the way I was living my life.

In my experience, the same logic applies to the homosexual dream encounters of heterosexual dreamers (I cannot speak to whether or not the same logic applies to dreams of homosexuals of heterosexual encounters). In the case of dreams of homosexual acts, there may be shadow elements involved (see the next section). Some of the more powerful dreams of sexual encounters that I've had symbolized my acceptance within myself of the qualities each dream character represented to me. I judge that to be a good sign, a sign that my dream is telling me something positive about the way I'm integrating those qualities into myself. These alter-gender issues bring us to the next set of images I wish to address.

Anima/Animus

> I dream I'm at a conference at a large campus that has a large grassy square in the middle. I'm off to one side at a counter or reception desk, like the maitre d' at a restaurant. There is a young woman there whose face is not very attractive, but she is very warm and friendly, very helpful—she has a good personality for that position. I'm quite attracted to her. She has been helping me get information.

14. Meier and Wise, *Windows of the Soul*, 188.

The dream images of the anima and animus are originally from Jung and his followers. I find myself increasingly drawn to this approach as I work with my own dreams and with the dreams of others in dream groups. Here is Jung's definition of these two terms:

> I was greatly intrigued by the fact that a woman should inter-
> fere with me from within. My conclusion was that she must be
> the "soul," in the primitive sense, and I began to speculate on the
> reasons why the name "anima" was given to the soul. Why was it
> thought of as feminine? Later I came to see that this inner femi-
> nine figure plays a typical, or archetypal, role in the unconscious
> of a man, and I called her the "anima." The corresponding figure in
> the unconscious of a woman I called the "animus."[15]

Several years ago I began looking for anima figures in my dreams. I created a chart listing each dream that had an anima figure, along with the
date, dream title, significant actions, and some initial personal reflections. I
found it a very fruitful endeavor that took my dream life in a new direction.
The partial dream narrated above is one of those where I attributed anima
energy, or soul energy, to a character. The character was not familiar to me
at all, and this anonymity helped me to recognize the character as anima
energy. For women, the animus characters come into play in a similar fashion. This kind of work is the beginning of a journey to wholeness or, to give
the concept a more traditional religious spin, to holiness. Hall and Nordby
explain this process as follows:

> If the personality is to be well adjusted and harmoniously balanced,
> the feminine side of a man's personality and the masculine side
> of a woman's personality must be allowed to express themselves
> in consciousness and behavior. If a man exhibits only masculine
> traits, his feminine traits remain unconscious and therefore these
> traits remain undeveloped and primitive. This gives the uncon-
> scious a quality of weakness and impressionability. That is why
> the most virile-appearing and virile-acting man is often weak and
> submissive inside. A woman who exhibits excessive femininity
> in her external life would have the unconscious qualities of stub-
> bornness or willfulness, qualities that are often present in man's
> outer behavior.[16]

---

15. Jung, *Memories, Dreams, Reflections,* 186.
16. Hall and Nordby, *A Primer of Jungian Psychology,* 46–47.

The process of finding and working with your anima or animus characters leads to the balance suggested here. We will be more whole people, more holy people, when we achieve that balance in our waking life that our dreams invite us towards. Now I will address the next image, that of the shadow. As Hoss notes, "The shadow figure in dreams is always the same sex as the dreamer. Otherwise a character functioning the same way of the opposite sex is anima or animus."[17]

The Shadow

I dream I am observing two black families having dinner together. One of the men spouts bigotry while the children of the other man watch. The second man responds gently, out of love, and says he no longer wants to be a character in a TV script, with typical white fears being projected onto him. I'm very moved by the compassion and love that seem to be part of this second man's response.

The "shadow" part of our dream work has to do with the parts of ourselves that we tend to repress, to keep from public view, because these parts are less acceptable in the society in which we live.[18] The shadow parts of us are different from how we like to think of ourselves. In the dream described above, my shadow character—actually, two aspects of it—is a person with black skin (in real life, I am a white man). I think of this dream as an example of a dream telling a joke; in case I didn't understand that these two men were shadow parts of myself, the dream painted them as black men!

The concept of the shadow is an important part of the thought of Carl Jung, and it has entered the popular vocabulary in relation to human psychology. Jung notes that he encountered and worked with elements of his own shadow in his younger days through his reading of Goethe's *Faust:*

> *Faust* struck a chord in me and pierced me through in a way that I could not but regard as personal. Most of all, it awakened in me the problem of opposites, of good and evil, of mind and matter, of light and darkness. Faust, the inept, purblind philosopher, encounters the dark side of his being, his sinister shadow, Mephistopheles, who in spite of his negating disposition represents the

17. Hoss, *Dream Language*, 96.

18. Robert A. Johnson phrases it this way: "[The shadow is] that dumping ground for all those characteristics of our personality that we disown." Johnson, *Owning Your Own Shadow*, ix.

true spirit of life as against the arid scholar who hovers on the brink of suicide.[19]

I believe the shadow concept is most helpful in looking at relationships between people, particularly those of differing races, languages, ethnicities, and cultures. Using the shadow concept in this way is standard in the world of dream work. The following examples help explain this concept, as well as why it is so helpful in dream work:

- "It is a dark page in human history when people make others bear their shadow for them. Men lay their shadow upon women, whites upon blacks, Catholics upon Protestants, capitalists upon communists, Muslims upon Hindus."[20]

- "What was the source of the Salem witch-hunts? What produced the character assassinations of the McCarthy era? Why can seemingly loving Christian people turn on each other with the vengeance of man-eating tigers? Hate, suspicion, paranoid distrust, gossip—the viciousness of accusers lurks in their own souls like a hidden terrible infection, a psychological time bomb poised to explode. When the right target crosses their paths, a volcanic eruption follows."[21]

Bulkeley offers a notable contemporary application of the shadow concept:

> In the days immediately following September 11, President Bush and virtually every other government official spoke out against racial profiling and prejudice against Muslims, Arabs, Middle Easterners, or anyone who simply "looked like a terrorist." Speaking at the Islamic Center of Washington, D.C., President Bush said, "America counts millions of Muslims amongst our citizens, and Muslims make an incredibly valuable contribution to our country. . . . And they need to be treated with respect. In our anger and emotion, our fellow Americans must treat each other with respect." . . . The terror Americans felt in response to September 11 could not help but trigger intense, primal fears aimed at anyone who even remotely resembled the people responsible for the attack. This kind of knee-jerk prejudice is, of course, itself a source

19. Jung, *Memories, Dreams, Reflections*, 235.
20. Johnson, *Owning Your Own Shadow*, 32.
21. Meier and Wise, *Windows of the Soul*, 219.

of terrible injustice, and that was the exact point of the comments from President Bush and the others.[22]

John Sanford, an Episcopal priest and Jungian analyst, describes the value of the shadow concept by alluding to the words of Jesus in Matt 5:25 in what might be considered a psychological reading of the gospel:

> The problem of the shadow demands both psychological insight and spiritual perspective, if it is to be solved. At the level of the dream, psychology and religion are inseparable. . . . Jung said about our collective shadow that it is 90 percent pure gold. Without a contact with our shadow we would become self-righteous, devoid of life, lacking in human understanding, sexually cold, unable to have living relationships with people, cut off from the earth, just plain dull, and subject to unconscious cruelties of a frightful proportion.[23]

This interpretation of Scripture points out the value of our shadow.[24] Johnson, too, discusses the importance of working with the shadow images in dreams. He believes that to honor and accept one's own shadow is a profound spiritual discipline. It is whole-making and thus holy, and it is the most important experience of one's lifetime.[25]

Nightmares

I dream I'm in a car with a childhood friend at the wheel and my 11-year-old son in the back seat. We've been driving around an area that is high on a hill. We drive into a cul-de-sac with an open lot to the right, ahead of us. I look down the slope and can see little rock outcroppings, one large enough for someone to sit on, but I cannot see the bottom. My friend starts to turn the car around to drive out, but at the point where the back end is pointing to the empty lot, the car starts to slide backwards, and he is not able to get the car moving

---

22. Bulkeley, *Dreams of Healing*, 115.

23. Sanford, *Dreams: God's Forgotten Language*, 41. Sanford found this concept of integrating one's shadow so important that he named the first chapter of his book "Agree with Thine Adversary."

24. This kind of psychological interpretation is one of the many levels at which the Christian scriptures may be read. In my work as a lectionary preacher, which means I preached on the same specific biblical passages every few years, I found it very helpful to be able to preach about different levels of meaning in the biblical texts.

25. Johnson, *Owning Your Own Shadow*, x.

forward again. We slide over the edge and start falling down backwards. I figure we will hit some bushes, etc., soon, but we don't—we keep falling straight down, gathering speed, and I know the crash will be a big and serious one.

I awoke from this dream quite upset, which lasted a few moments until I realized it was a dream. Then, I realized this nightmare might be offering me a form of healing.

One of the most enlightening insights I have gained from studying dreams is that nightmares are really messages of healing. This is one of those concepts that one needs to experience to realize its full truth. What initially frightens the dreamer can become a source of help and strength. Taylor has this to say about nightmares:

> When the unconscious has particularly important information to convey to the waking mind, our dreams are very likely to assume nasty, negative, "nightmarish" forms *simply to grab and hold our attention.* Nightmares, like all other dreams, come in the service of the dreamer's health and wholeness.[26]

Taylor goes on to describe how dreams will repeat themselves until the underlying issue that is prompting the dream is dealt with. The dreams will get increasingly more frightening in an escalation of the attempt to get the dreamer's attention. This idea, too, can offer comfort when one has a nightmare.[27]

> *I'm leading a Christmas, Easter, or other big service in a place like my current church, but it's arranged differently than in real life. I completely forget to do the announcements, and I don't even have them printed out. I feel really bad about this and leave the chapel feeling greatly ashamed and embarrassed.*

One of the recurring dreams I noticed in my initial years of reflecting on my dreams was what I came to call the "preacher's nightmare," similar to the one described above. I've found that teachers, public speakers, and others who deliver talks to groups of people all report having had such dreams. This is Taylor's take on such dreams or nightmares:

26. Taylor, *The Living Labyrinth*, 50, italics in original.

27. Hedberg says: "One of the best and most comforting things I've learned is that if you don't get a dream message the first or second or third time around—either because you haven't had time to work on the dream, or because it just won't let itself be unlocked—the message will keep coming until you do get it—IF you've made the time commitment we're talking about." Caprio and Hedberg, *At a Dream Workshop*, 106.

In my experience, this generic dream also reflects the dreamer's spiritual predicament. It is as though every person were automatically enrolled in an ongoing "class" at birth called something like "What Is Really Going On Here Below the Surface of Mere Appearance." Over the course of living our lives, we "forget" that answering this question is one of our primary commitments and obligations. Every once in a while, the fact that we have neglected this psychospiritual inquiry and that a "final exam" is coming up (at every developmental milestone and ultimately at death) shakes our conventional attitude, and we tend to have some version of the dream.[28]

Gosh, and I thought I was just anxious about forgetting to make some announcements!

Familiar Characters

I need to make one final comment about characters in dreams. I was asked a question by a woman in a demonstration dream group about why family members showed up so seldom in her dreams. My response was that we are so busy in our daily waking lives interacting with family members that we are constantly working through whatever issues we might have with them. We need to address these issues while awake in order to get along in our everyday relationships with family and current friends. In our dreams, though, we are working through deeper or different issues, ones that are more directly related to our interior lives. The characters in our dreams have more to do with ourselves and our inner dynamics. The difference here is that dream images are symbolic. So, when we dream about a character whom we knew at some distant past point in our lives, our dream work is more likely to benefit us if we ask ourselves what about that character and our relationship with that person is similar to a situation we might now be facing in our waking life. This is different from dreaming about something that took place yesterday or three days ago in the presence of a family member or a friend with whom we have a current active relationship. See the discussion of dream classification in chapter 1.

28. Taylor, *The Living Labyrinth*, 164.

Jesus in Dreams

One of the most interesting areas of the dream experiences of Christians has to do with why many Christians who do dream work have very few dreams with Jesus in them. During the one-year period when I closely studied dream groups in churches, only one person in all the groups had a single dream with Jesus in it. I've yet to run across any literature about dreams that addresses this specific issue. Is it a common experience that Jesus does not show up in the dreams of Christians? If so, what might be the reason?

I discussed this topic with Dr. G. Scott Sparrow at the International Association for the Study of Dreams (IASD) conference in Massachusetts in June of 2006. His book *Sacred Encounters with Jesus* includes discussions of people's experiences of meeting Jesus in dreams and visions. I shared my experiences, or lack of experiences, of Jesus in dreams over lunch one day. He replied that he had found that Jesus only showed up in a dream when the dreamer was desperate, when it seemed there was no other help to be had except divine intervention. Theologically, this makes sense to me. Jesus will not do for us what we can and should do for ourselves.

My only dream about Jesus was one in which I was playing golf with Jesus. I dreamt this in seminary, soon after I began keeping track of my dreams. I understood the dream to be telling me I needed to get more rest and recreation, not to study so hard. I hardly needed Jesus to tell me that, though. So, why was Jesus in that dream? Maybe it was a way to let me know of the power and usefulness of my dreams. I cannot say for sure, but this one remembered experience of Jesus in my dreams adds to my desire to know more about what seems to me to be an unexplained absence of Jesus as a character in my own dreams. My faith life makes frequent references to Jesus, yet my thirty-plus years of dream recall and dream work contains only this one, enigmatic reference to the person I consider my Lord and Savior.

When I've raised this issue at IASD conferences, some people respond that maybe Jesus does appear in dreams—but as an archetypal figure giving wisdom or comfort or inspiration. I view this response as coming from a Jungian perspective in which Jesus is seen as no more than a psychological archetype. I believe Jesus is more than just an archetype. Because Jesus is so significant in Christianity, the focus of so many stories in Scripture and so many works of art, I would expect more reports of dreams that have Jesus specifically in them.

This brief discussion of some of the images and characters in dreams is designed to improve dreamers' understanding of their dreams. The negative associations that we have in our waking lives with death, immoral sex, shadow characters, and nightmares all have the potential to be helpful in tending our dreams. As Taylor says, all dreams come in the service of health and wholeness. "The more distressing the image, the greater the gift it hides below the ugly surface of its appearance."[29] I hope this brief survey of some of the more prevalent dream images points the reader toward a better understanding of that expression.

One point that I may not have stressed sufficiently is the importance of the reaction of the dreamer to whatever the image is. If the "aha" moment of recognition is not there for the dreamer, all the symbol theories in the world don't matter. This is one of the problems with the dream dictionaries that are for sale at grocery store check-out counters (I will say more about these symbol dictionaries in chapter 9).[30] Dreams speak a different language than we are accustomed to speaking in our culture, but it is a comprehensible language with meaning and coherence. The language of dreams is an ancient language. It is a language that anyone can learn to understand.

29. Ibid., 73.

30. Hoss notes, "A dream 'dictionary' may simply contain the author's own personal associations or a collection of associations derived from other sources. Although you may connect with a few of the dream 'dictionary' metaphors, there is no way that a 'dictionary' can determine the true personal content within your dream image. Only the dreamer can provide that information." Hoss, *Dream Language,* 57.

5

Dreams in the Bible

Now the birth of Jesus the Messiah took place in this way. When his mother Mary had been engaged to Joseph, but before they lived together, she was found to be with child from the Holy Spirit. Her husband Joseph, being a righteous man and unwilling to expose her to public disgrace, planned to dismiss her quietly. But just when he had resolved to do this, an angel of the Lord appeared to him in a dream and said, "Joseph, son of David, do not be afraid to take Mary as your wife, for the child conceived in her is from the Holy Spirit. She will bear a son, and you are to name him Jesus, for he will save his people from their sins." All this took place to fulfill what had been spoken by the Lord through the prophet:

"Look, the virgin shall conceive and bear a son,
and they shall name him Emmanuel,"

which means, "God is with us." When Joseph awoke from sleep, he did as the angel of the Lord commanded him; he took her as his wife, but had no marital relations with her until she had borne a son; and he named him Jesus.

—Matt 1:18–25[1]

T he Bible contains several stories related to dreams and the influence dreams had on biblical characters. The above story from Matthew 1 is probably the best-known dream story in the New Testament. This story of Jesus' birth and early life is full of dreams that guide the characters and protect Jesus from before his birth through his early years. It is one of sev-

---

1. All quotations from the Bible in this chapter are from the New Revised Standard Version (NRSV).

eral dream stories in Scripture. These stories and their references to dreams are important in understanding the roles dreams have played in the lives of Christians over the centuries. In this chapter, I look at the Old and New Testaments and some of the dreams and dream characters found there, and in the next chapter I examine dreams in the history of the Christian church. Here, I focus on examples of how the use of dreams by characters in the biblical narratives might help us in our work with dreams.

The world of the Bible and the contemporary world are quite different, particularly when it comes to the technologies that humans use to achieve their cultural goals. But human existence and human characteristics have not changed greatly from the biblical era to our time. Dreams have been with us since the beginning of human existence. Dreams and dreaming are universal, so the experience of dreaming is not that different now than it was in the ancient world. What has changed, however, is our attitude toward dreams.

In addition to stories about dreams, numerous stories of visions and revelations received by biblical characters are recounted in the Bible. Visions and revelations have many characteristics in common with dreams. For the purposes of this book, I am using the classic definition of a dream as an experience that comes to us during sleep. Visions and revelations seem to come only to certain people. Dreams, on the other hand, are universally and readily available. The premise of this book is that we can use these universally available dreams in our lives of faith. In the following two sections, I point out parallels between our dreams and those of biblical characters.

Old Testament

The Old Testament has several dream stories. Some of the stories support the idea of dreams as vehicles of divine communication, but others offer harsh criticism to those who pay attention to dreams. We will look at some of these dreams and their critics in the Bible. The outstanding dreams in the Old Testament are those of Jacob and Joseph in Genesis and those of Daniel in the book of the same name.

The first dream of substance in the Old Testament is the dream of Jacob, recounted in Gen 28. There are dreams in earlier chapters, however, notably that of Abimelech in chapter 20. Some of the visionary experiences related to Abraham in 15:1 and 18:2 might be considered dreams, but the focus here is on texts that refer to a dream as a night vision that occurs during sleep. Jacob's dream of the ladder plays a very important role in his life and has been popular with Bible readers throughout the ages. It is a dream specifically about contact between heaven and earth, about communication between the divine and human realms. This kind of contact has been desired by many people in many different times and cultures. That is the purpose of prayer and many devotional practices—to open the channel of communication between the divine and the human.

In Gen 28, Jacob is under some stress as he lies down to sleep one night. He has been sent by his father to find a wife among his mother's relatives, which is certainly a time when most people would want some kind of guidance. We don't know if Jacob asked for a dream or prayed for guidance as he went to sleep, which is what we might do in a similar situation. What we do know is that Jacob received a dream that was a powerful experience. It was so powerful that Jacob recognized it as a communication from God and memorialized the location with a ritual. The location later became Bethel, the site of the first religious shrine in Israel. *Bethel* means "house of God," signifying the religious significance of this place where God spoke to one of the patriarchs of Israel in a dream.

Looking more closely at this dream offers us insights for the use of dreams in our own spiritual lives. None of the vision itself—the ladder, the angels moving up and down the ladder, the presence of God speaking to the dreamer—is out of line with the general characteristics of dreams as described in the previous chapters of this book. What we might consider for our own use is how Jacob responds to his dream. First of all, he recognizes it as an important dream, a big dream in his life. He considers this dream a gate to heaven, clearly a communication from God. But, I want to emphasize how Jacob acts in response to the dream. He sets up a little altar to memorialize his experience at that place. If we, like Jacob, act in response to our dreams, we will incorporate our dreams more thoroughly into our lives. Suggestions for ways to do this will be covered in more detail in chapter 9. Most of the recipients of dreams in the Bible act on their dreams in some way.

Another famous dreamer in the Old Testament is Joseph, son of Jacob. The stories of Joseph are found in Genesis chapters 37 to 50. Joseph is involved in dreams at two significant periods in his life. When he is still a youth in chapter 37, his dreams become a source of tension between him and his brothers; in fact, Joseph and his brothers have to wait years before they are able to recognize the insights the dreams brought. Then, after the dream-engendered envy of his brothers lands Joseph in Egypt, Joseph's dreams come to his aid, and based on his dreams Joseph rescues Egypt and Israel from famine (Gen 40–42).

Joseph's role changes from dreamer to dream interpreter as he works with the dreams of Pharaoh. Joseph had learned enough from his own dream experiences to apply his learning and wisdom to the dreams of those around him. Like his father Jacob before him, what Joseph does with the dream of Pharaoh makes a difference. Interpreting a dream can be risky, but Joseph takes the risk and saves the lives of countless Egyptians—and of his own family. He acts on his and others' dreams and makes decisions based on those dreams. That is the type of work with dreams that is available to us all, though perhaps not with such dramatic results.

The dreams in the book of Daniel are found in chapters 1, 2, 4, and 7. Daniel performs the role of dream interpreter, much like Joseph did. These stories suggest that dreams and dream interpretation are simply one of several ways in which God communicates with the people of God. In the book of Daniel, the narrative reveals that Daniel's god is more powerful and wise than the Babylonian gods. This is an example of dreams being used to proclaim the one true God of Israel. There are noticeable parallels between the characters and situations of Daniel and Joseph. They are both in service to a Gentile ruler, they are both skilled in understanding the spiritual aspects of dreams, and they both bring glory to the God of Israel. And, significantly, both Joseph and Daniel take specific action based on their dreams.

The Old Testament contains some explicit statements about dreams. On the positive side, Job 33:15–16 says this about God:

> In a dream, in a vision of the night,
>
> When deep sleep falls on mortals,
>
> While they slumber on their beds,
>
> Then he opens their ears
>
> And terrifies them with warnings.

The "he" in line four refers to God. The last line of this text seems to be referring more to nightmares than the wide variety of types of dreams that people experience (see chapter 1). For our purposes, though, this text points to the use of dreams by the God of Israel as one of the many ways God communicates with believers. I find it interesting that the specific sense organ that is referred to here is the ear. Hearing sounds in dreams is an exceptional event, not normal. Most dreams are visual and emotional. I believe the reference to hearing in this text comes from the Hebrew culture of the time, where hearing God's word was a more normal way for human-divine communication to occur than it is today for most Christians. There is no apparent judgment on whether dreams and their uses are positive or negative in this example from Job. Dreams are simply acknowledged as a valid way for God to speak.

Numbers 12:6–7 also contains a rather straightforward statement about God using dreams to communicate with humans:

> When there are prophets among you,
>
> I the Lord make myself known to them in visions,
>
> I speak to them in dreams.
>
> Not so with my servant Moses . . .

The text goes on to talk about the superiority of Moses and the fact that God spoke face-to-face with Moses, not indirectly or in riddles or images, as in dreams and visions. Like the example from Job, the value of dreams and the use of dreams as a communication medium for God are accepted in this text from Numbers.

A more negative attitude towards dreams and dreaming is evident in certain other texts in the Old Testament. Deuteronomy 13:1–5 contains these words about dreams:

> If prophets or those who divine by dreams appear among you and promise you omens or portents, and the omens or portents declared by them take place, and they say "Let us follow other gods" (whom you have not known) "and let us serve them" . . . those prophets or those who divine by dreams shall be put to death for having spoken treason against the Lord your God.

Death to those who deal in dreams! That is strong language and seems to run contrary to the texts cited above that give a more positive cast to the use of dreams in one's life of faith. The prophet Jeremiah has some strong words against dreaming, too:

> I have heard what the prophets have said who prophesy lies in my name, saying, "I have dreamed, I have dreamed." How long? Will the hearts of the prophets ever turn back—those who prophesy lies, and who prophesy the deceit of their own heart? They plan to make my people forget my name by their dreams that they tell one another. . . . Let the prophet who has a dream tell the dream, but let the one who has my word speak my word faithfully. What

has straw in common with wheat? . . . See, I am against those who
prophesy lying dreams, says the Lord, and who tell them, and
who lead my people astray by their lies and their recklessness. (Jer
23:25–32)

These passages from Deuteronomy and Jeremiah remind us that
dreams are not always used in healthy ways and to the benefit of others. But
a close reading of both of these passages shows that it is not so much the
dreams and dreaming itself that are condemned as it is the use of dreams
to draw people away from the God of Israel. That is a crucial distinction. In
both passages the phenomenon of using dreams to claim divine wisdom,
and perhaps the special privilege that might go along with that wisdom,
seems to be at work. This is always a problem with those who use dreams
for their own ends, and there are examples of such misuse of dreams in our
own day. But the condemnation expressed in these passages is aimed at
those activities that draw people away from God. This distinction helps us
keep a balance between the positive use of dreams, as seen in the books of
Genesis, Daniel, Job, and Numbers, and the negative use of dreams referred
to in Deuteronomy and Jeremiah. More about some of these specific texts
can be found in chapter 6, where I look at the Protestant Reformers Luther
and Calvin and their attitudes towards dreams.

Another possible reference to dreams is found in the book of Psalms.
The psalms have long been a rich source of devotional material for both Jews
and Christians, and the book of Psalms has been called "the prayer book
of the Bible." Christian movements and traditions such as the Benedictine
Order and various Protestant denominations use the psalms for daily devo-
tions. The psalms do not contain any specific references to dreams, but the
wording of some verses might be interpreted in that way. Take Ps 16:7:

> I will bless the Lord who gives me counsel;
>
> My heart teaches me, night after night.

In my study of the psalms, I've not found a commentator who refers to this
verse as possibly speaking about dreams. Yet the phrase "teachings of my
heart at night" is a great description of dreams. Likewise, in Ps 19:2,

> One day tells its tale to another,
>
> And one night imparts knowledge to another.

The "knowledge that comes at night" could be referring to the knowledge
that dreams pass on to us, night after night. This description fits very well

with my understanding of what dreams and dreaming do for us. These verses in the psalms tie into dreams nicely and provide excellent alternate definitions of dreams and dreaming. I will talk more about the psalms—their harsh images as well as my personal use of the psalms in my devotional life—in chapter 7.

A positive reference to dreams is found in the life of Solomon, who was the son of and successor to King David. Solomon is popularly known for his wisdom, but less well known is the method by which Solomon attained his wisdom. Dream incubation is a method of fostering dreams or requesting dreams that speak about a particular issue. Dream incubation techniques are found in many ancient and primitive cultures, and many rituals have been developed to prompt a dream that addresses the particular concern of the dreamer. In 1 Kgs 3, God appeared to Solomon in a dream:

> 4The king went to Gibeon to sacrifice there, for that was the principal high place; Solomon used to offer a thousand burnt offerings of that altar. 5At Gibeon the Lord appeared to Solomon in a dream by night; and God said, "Ask what I should give you." . . . 9[Solomon responded,] "Give your servant therefore an understanding mind to govern your people, able to discern between good and evil; for who can govern this your great people." . . . 15Then Solomon woke; it had been a dream. He came to Jerusalem where he stood before the ark of the covenant of the Lord. He offered up burnt offerings and offerings of well-being, and provided a feast for all his servants.

In contemporary terms, Solomon uses incubation in verses 4 and 5, meaning he sets an intention to get help from God. That help is given in a dream (verse 9 is part of the request), and then Solomon acts on the basis of his dream in verse 15. This is one of the most solid ways to work dreams from a modern perspective and will be further described in chapter 10.

The biblical book Song of Songs, also known as the Song of Solomon, contains specific references to dreams. The NRSV calls 3:1–5 a dream scene, likely based upon the opening words, "Upon my bed at night." The activity of dreaming can be inferred from this wording. Another example is found in chapter 5:2: "I slept, but my heart was awake." That could be a good definition of dreaming—we are asleep, but our heart continues functioning. Indeed, modern brain physiology confirms that while we are sleeping, our brains are active, sometimes expending greater energy while asleep than while awake (see chapter 1). Our hearts are awake, indeed!

New Testament

The New Testament contains fewer accounts of dreams than the Old Testament. Part of the reason may be that it is shorter in length than the Old Testament and covers a shorter time span. But, the role that dreams and dreaming play in the New Testament is just as important as in the Old Testament. The specific places where dreams are found are the birth stories of Jesus as described in the gospels of Matthew and Luke.

The story of the announcement to Mary that she would bear the messiah in Luke 1 is the first event in the birth narratives that pertains specifically to Jesus. This is not referred to as a dream, but the parallels between this event and the dream of Jacob in Genesis are noteworthy. Mary's experience is portrayed as a meeting of heaven and earth, of the spiritual and the material, similar to what occurs in the dream of Jacob in Gen 28. For Jacob it is a stream of angels ascending and descending the ladder between heaven and earth. For Mary it is only one angel, though a very important one.

By far the most important dream stories in the New Testament that are clearly called dreams are those related to the birth and protection of the baby Jesus in Matthew's gospel. These stories are so intertwined with popular Christmas stories that it is easy to overlook the fact that these are dream stories that are taken very seriously by the characters involved. These dream stories are in the first two chapters of Matthew, as follows:

1:20	Joseph is told in a dream to take Mary as his wife, despite her scandalous pregnancy.
2:12	The wise men are warned in a dream not to return to Herod.
2:13	Joseph is warned in a dream to flee to Egypt.
2:19–20	Joseph is told in a dream that he can return to Israel.
2:22	Joseph is warned in another dream to go to Galilee, not Judea.

The above passages are five instances in just a few verses in which dreams play a major role in protecting God's plan and Jesus and his family. The theology of Matthew's gospel plays a role here. Some scholars argue that the author of Matthew was seeking to influence the direction that Judaism was taking after the destruction of Jerusalem by the Romans. Jewish leaders saw the need for reform as a consequence of the destruction of Jerusalem.

Matthew sought to place Jesus at the center of faith instead of the laws and rules that were being put forward by those within Judaism. For contemporary people interested in using dreams in our lives of faith, the valuable point in these dream narratives from the first two chapters of Matthew's gospel is the seriousness with which the dreams are taken. Joseph and the wise men appear to have no hesitation in taking the dreams as guides in the situations in which they find themselves. Would that we would have such clarity about the meaning of our dreams and the directions they give us!

The other interesting point is that the dreams are not just taken seriously; they are also acted upon—immediately. Joseph is ready to quietly divorce his intended bride, no doubt a painful and shameful decision. But his dream is enough for him to change his mind and risk the shame that he would be subjected to. The wise men, too, change their itinerary as a consequence of their dream. Their dream provides a map, as it were, that does not show them where to go but does at least show them where *not* to go. The same can be said for the next three dreams in Matthew, all of which guide Joseph in his travels.

Acting upon our dreams is very important. These dreams in the opening of Matthew's gospel show the way acting on our dreams can make a difference in our lives. These chapters in Matthew are an invitation to trust our dreams, trust in the messages and in the alternate views of life and perspectives on daily events that they offer.

These selections from the Bible show the role that dreams play in several sacred texts of Jews, Christians, and Muslims. Upon looking closely at these texts, it becomes clear that our culture has devalued dreams and dreaming. As a consequence, references to dreams in biblical material are often overlooked in discussions of models for Christian practice. The Bible gives an accurate portrait of the human soul throughout time. We in the twenty-first century are much more sophisticated in our view of the world and know more about the hows and whys of life on earth than those who lived in biblical times. Yet, according to the Christian church, as well as the other religions that rely on the Bible, the insights of the Bible are just as relevant today as they were two thousand years ago in relation to the picture of the human soul that they portray. One of the interesting insights that some people gain as they work with their dreams is that their dreams are not very different from the dreams that are narrated in the Bible. That is one of the benefits I feel we can achieve through working with our dreams.

Whatever we can do to make the Bible come more alive in our daily lives is worth doing. Dream work is one of the ways to foster this.

As we come to a deeper understanding of the limits of our rationalistic worldview developed over the last few centuries, we may look for new ways to explore our faith. The Bible provides us with a faithful map of human life and God's interaction with humans that the church has proclaimed for all its history. Particularly for those of us in the Protestant tradition, reliance upon the Bible is a key element in grounding our faith in tradition. Although the Bible does not tell us how to use our own dreams, it does treat seriously the dreams of the characters in the Bible, and thus it provides an example that we can follow in our own dream work.

6

Dreams in the History of the Church

One man learns . . . while awake, another while asleep. But in the waking state man is the teacher, whereas it is God who makes the dreamer fruitful with His own courage, so that learning and attaining are one and the same.

—Synesius of Cyrene (ca. 373–414)

Synesius was a bishop of Ptolemais in the early years of the fifth century, and one of his major writings was about the causes and meanings of dreams. Synesius suggested ways of working with dreams that were forerunners of many modern dream work practices. For example, he suggested that people keep a record of their dreams and use their dreams to help them find inspiration and identify communications from God. He also discouraged people from using the popular dream books of the day. Synesius's work shows that the contemporary variety of uses and understandings of dreams is not particular to our time and culture.

The Christian church has been of two minds about dreams. The church has either taken dreams seriously as vehicles of God's revelations to humans or dismissed them as figments of the imagination, physical reactions to food eaten the night before, or visions given by the devil to seduce worthy people away from God. In its early years, the church vacillated between seeking respectability and drawing on its prophetic and mystical heritage. When church leaders sought respectability, they would push concerns with mystical elements, including dreams, off to the side in order to appear stable and mainstream. When they attended to the church's prophetic and mystical heritage, the church was relegated to the margins of society. This tension has remained in the church until the present day and, presumably, will remain into the foreseeable future.[1] In this chapter I will dip into various times and places in the history of the Christian church to illustrate the role that dreams have played over the course of Christian history.

The determining factor regarding whether and how dreams are used by faithful Christians is the understanding of where dreams come from. The biblical examples cited in the previous chapter refer to dreams that come from God. There are some references in the Bible to other theories related to the sources of dreams, such as Jer 23:23–32. Christians over the centuries have sorted their theories about the sources of dreams into three general categories: God, demons, and (to use Aristotle's term) somatic sources. By *somatic* Aristotle means bodily influences, such as food we may have eaten the night before or external sounds while we are asleep, like traffic outside our bedroom or changes in temperature, as when our partner pulls the blankets off us and we get cold. Theories about the origins of dreams come and go with changes in culture as well as the changing circumstances the church finds itself in, but generally these same three theories about the sources of dreams have been proposed by the church over the centuries, with only minor variations. From the perspective of the church, if a dream comes from God, then it should be paid attention to. If it comes from the devil, it should be ignored—if not exorcised. If it just comes from something we ate last night, it probably means little and we are wasting our time paying attention to it and trying to gain insight or meaning from it.

The earliest work on dreams in the nascent Christian church is that of Tertullian (ca. 160–225). Tertullian was an African Church Father who spent most of his life in and around Carthage, one of the centers of early Christianity. He had considerable influence upon early Christian thought, so much so that he has been called the father of Latin theology. His influence is most noticeable in the work of Cyprian and Augustine of Hippo. It is suspected that Tertullian edited *The Passion of Perpetua and Felicity*, one of the most powerful and inspirational texts of the early church. Dreams played a major role in the story of these two female martyrs.[2]

1. I am indebted to the work of Morton Kelsey, whose book *God, Dreams, and Revelation* was originally published in 1968, for much of the material in this chapter. Perhaps more than anyone else, Kelsey's work reintroduced the history of dreams to the modern Christian church, as well as the possibility of using dreams in one's life of faith.

2. See Davis, "The Weaning of Perpetua." Davis treats this ancient dream of Perpetua, which played a role in the martyrdom of early Christians, with contemporary tools of dream interpretation.

Tertullian categorizes dreams based on their source, as follows:

1. From demons: Most dreams come from demons, although these dreams "sometimes turn out true and favorable to us."

2. From God: "Almost the greater part of mankind get [sic] their knowledge of God from dreams."

3. Natural dreams: The soul creates these dreams for itself from "an intense application to special circumstances."

4. Dreams that come from none of the above sources must be ascribed to "what is purely and simply the ecstatic state and its peculiar conditions."[3]

This is the same three-fold pattern outlined earlier, except that Tertullian replaces Aristotle's category of somatic dreams with natural and ecstatic dreams.

In his preface to *The Martyrdom of Perpetua and Felicitas*, Tertullian makes an important point. In reference to Joel 2, he notes that this kind of revelation was still taking place, although it is difficult to tell whether he is referring specifically to dreams in this passage. Then Tertullian suggests that these "modern visions" be collected in writing and commemorated to God's glory.[4] This is the type of dream work that I have found most helpful. Early Christians, however, were not wholeheartedly and unanimously in favor of using dreams. Cyprian, a student of Tertullian, mentions that there was ambivalence about dreams in his time. He notes that some people rejected the idea that dreams might have any meaning simply because dreams were valued by church leaders, but he also refers to several people and places where dreams were valued as having great importance in the religious life.

A major turning point in the history of Christianity came with the conversion of Constantine in the year 303 CE. It is significant that this conversion came about through a dream. Constantine was about to engage in

---

3 Discussed in Kelsey, *Gods, Dreams and Revelation*, 109.

4. "And thus we—who both acknowledge and reverence, even as we do the prophecies, modern visions as equally promised to us, and consider the other powers of the Holy Spirit as an agency of the Church for which also He was sent, administering all gifts in all, even as the Lord distributed to every one as will needfully collect them in writing, and commemorate them in reading to God's glory; that so no weakness or despondency of faith may suppose that the divine grace abode only among the ancients, whether in respect of the condescension that raise up martyrs, or that gave revelations." Tertullian, *The Ante-Nicene Fathers*, 699.

a battle for the possession of the city of Rome, which would lead to his becoming the emperor of Rome, and he prayed for help. Constantine was not yet a Christian, but he meditated on "the attitude of his own father toward the one supreme God" and, as the saying goes, the rest is history. Through a combination of a waking vision and dream confirmation, Constantine had his soldiers paint crosses on their shields, and because they won the battle Constantine decided that he would adopt Christianity, the faith of the cross.[5] As a result, the Christian church was allowed to move into the mainstream of Roman society.

As the Christian church became accepted in Roman society, the role of dreams was marginalized by most within the church. Kelsey cites one exception to this, the early Father Synesius of Cyrene, whose statement on the democracy of dreaming is significant. Dreams can be helpful tools in our spiritual lives because dreams happen to us regularly and are universally available—in other words, everyone dreams. In the words of Synesius:

> But the dream is visible to the man who is worth five hundred *medimni*, and equally to the possessor of three hundred, to the teamster no less than to the peasant who tills the boundary land for a livelihood, to the galley slave and the common laborer alike, to the exempted and to the payer of taxes.[6]

Dreams during the Protestant Reformation

The Christian church experienced a schism in the sixteenth century as a result of the Protestant Reformation. Two major figures in this reform movement were Martin Luther, the founder of the Lutheran denomination of Christianity, and John Calvin, the founder of the Reformed denominations. Both Luther and Calvin had tremendous influence on Christianity, and their attitudes towards dreams are helpful in examining the history of the use of dreams by Christians.[7] One of the major purposes of the Protestant Reformation was a return to the Bible as the basis for how and why things were to be done in the Christian church. In regard to dreams, this presented something of a problem for Luther, although less so for Calvin.

5. Kelsey, *Gods, Dreams and Revelation*, 116–17.

6. Quoted in ibid., 247.

7. I address this topic in more detail in Nelson, "Dreaming through the Bible with Luther and Calvin."

Dreams play a significant, though not major, role in the Bible. Therefore, dreams need to be taken seriously if the Bible is to be taken seriously. I will take a brief look at what Luther and Calvin have to say about the value of dreams through their commentaries on biblical dream texts.[8]

The following comment by Martin Luther has direct bearing on the use of personal dreams in one's life of prayer. Luther scoffed at the vanity of monks and nuns who wrote down their dreams. He is commenting on the visit of angels to Lot in Gen 19:14.

> [Before the beginning of Luther's reformation,] much was written and said about the contemplative and the active life; and in the monasteries and convents monks and nuns who, on the whole, were very pious eagerly strove to have visions and revelations presented to them. Consequently, some even noted down all their dreams. Evidently they all waited for extraordinary illuminations without external means. What else is this than a desire to ascend into heaven without ladders? Consequently, these monks and nuns were very frequently deceived by delusions of the devil.

Luther is arguing here that paying attention to dreams is an attempt to achieve revelation through our own effort. But, this is not Luther's only perspective on dreams. In his commentary on Gen 40:19 (one of Joseph's dream interpretations while in prison in Egypt), Luther continues to reject the use of dreams in his own personal life in favor of Scripture, but he acknowledges that some dreams do seem to come from God.

> But other dreams, which do not have their origin from God, are ambiguous and deceptive. Therefore there is need of extraordinary wisdom to differentiate them.
>
> I . . . always asked the Lord not to send me dreams, visions or angels. For many fanatical spirits attacked me, one of whom boasted of dreams, another of visions, and another of revelations with which they were striving to instruct me. But I replied that I was not seeking such revelations and that if any were offered, I would put no trust in them. And I prayed ardently to God that He might give me the sure meaning and understanding of Holy Scripture. For if I have the Word, I know that I am proceeding on the right way and cannot easily be deceived or go wrong.

8. The quotes from Martin Luther's writings in this chapter are from Luther, *Luther's Works*, in which the commentary is arranged by biblical chapter and verse. The quotes from John Calvin are from Calvin, *John Calvin's Commentaries*, which is also arranged by biblical chapter and verse.

With their dreams the fanatics were trying to drive me, some in one way, others in another. Had I listened to any of them, it would certainly have been necessary to change the character of my doctrine 30 or 40 times. But when I rejected them all, they kept crying out that I was stubborn and headstrong, and they let me alone. Therefore I care nothing about visions and dreams. Although they seem to have a meaning, yet I despise them and am content with the sure meaning and trustworthiness of Holy Scripture.

Nevertheless, all dreams should not be completely despised, even though I take no pleasure in them. But the marks of true dreams must be observed. For an impression soon follows those that are sent by God, so that he who dreams cannot forget the dream; or if it has escaped him, it soon recurs, as can be seen in the history of Nebuchadnezzar. For a seed cast by God must bear its fruit.

There are virtually no polemics in John Calvin's commentaries on biblical passages concerning dreams. Commenting upon Jer 23:25–27 (one of the negative texts covered in the previous chapter), Calvin says this: "Dreams themselves are to be taken in a good sense, for God was wont to make himself known to his servants by dreams." Hence, Calvin viewed dreams "from above" in a favorable light.

The classification and evaluation of the source of dreams is important to people of faith. Luther and Calvin each had their own classification system, though both systems are rooted in the categories developed by previous thinkers, particularly certain classical Greek and Roman writers and early Christian Fathers. Both agree that dreams are one of the ways that God communicates with humans. Calvin, in commenting upon both of the Josephs who had dreams (the son of Jacob in the Old Testament and the "stepfather" of Jesus in the New Testament), says that dreams are either from God or from everyday or natural sources. Luther goes along with the general three-part classification noted at the opening of this chapter. For Luther, dreams are either from God, from the devil or demons, or from physical causes. By physical causes, Luther is referring to the blood humors, the classification system of human temperaments developed by the ancient Greeks and Romans.

Luther adds a second level of classification of dreams that differentiates between the dreams of public persons and private persons. By public persons, he means those in public authority, such as nobility or rulers, whose dreams he considers prophetic. In commenting on Gen 41:25, he writes, "There is no doubt, however, that this explanation greatly plagued all the wisest and most learned men in that kingdom. But they all sweat in vain, because the dreams of kings and public persons are prophecies and require the Holy Spirit as an interpreter." In contrast, in his commentary on Gen 28:16 and Jacob's interpretation of his dream, Luther states, "Accordingly, political dreams that are vague and without a foundation—that is, when the person is not a public functionary or in the government, and when the agitation and the analogy are not added—are good for nothing."

The attitude of Luther and Calvin toward dreams is a very minor point given the overall theological challenges they faced and their particular responses to those challenges. The extent to which they shaped the Protestant perspective on the Bible and theology is monumental. In relation to dreams, the two Reformers appear to agree that dreams are significant if they are functioning under the operation of the Holy Spirit. Luther, in commenting on Joel 2:28, outlines three kinds of divine illumination, one of which is dreams: "These, nevertheless, one understands when the Holy Spirit interprets them so that those who have seen them have no doubts that the dreams come from God." Calvin agrees, as evidenced by his comment on the dreams of the king of Babylon that the prophet Daniel is asked to interpret:

> When Daniel says the Magi, Astrologers, and the rest cannot explain to the king his dream, and are not suitable interpreters of it, the true reason is, because the dream was not natural and had nothing in common with human conjectures, but was the peculiar revelation of the Spirit.

One of the major points emphasized by these two great Reformers, Luther and Calvin, was the importance of one's practice of faith being in congruence with the Bible. The same applied to their understanding of the role and place of dreams. Thus, Luther, talking about the dream of Jacob's ladder in Gen 28, says,

> You must compare your dream with the Word. If your dream differs from what the Word itself states, you must remember that it is false and vain. But this dream of Jacob is in very beautiful agreement with the divine Word which he hears being sent down from heaven: "I am the Lord . . . etc."

The theological concerns of Luther and Calvin were quite different from ours today, and we should not rely too much on their attitude towards dreams as an encouragement for our use of dreams in our spiritual life.

Nevertheless, it is helpful to see that there was ambivalence towards dreams during this important time in the history of the Christian church. Some of the tensions and misgivings about dreams and dream work are the same now as they were during the time of Luther and Calvin.

Emanuel Swedenborg: A Man Out of Time

Emanuel Swedenborg (1688–1772) was a fascinating person in whose life dreams played a large role. Swedenborg was a man of his time in that he pursued knowledge in all the current scientific realms and made lasting contributions to the fields of geometry, chemistry, and metallurgy. But in his later years he began to be more interested in the relation of spirit to matter, and he became a leading but controversial religious thinker of his age. Significantly, dreams were the means by which Swedenborg launched himself into new fields of endeavor. His *Journal of Dreams* is interesting reading for anyone keeping a dream journal. Though Swedenborg comes to some different conclusions about his dreams than we might today, it is clear from the narrative style of his writing that his dreams were much like the dreams of people everywhere.

Swedenborg is an example of someone who moved very much in the rational world of scientific observation and experimentation but also moved in the more mythical or religious world. His writings have continued to be influential since his death.[9] Swedenborg was a man out of time because he was willing to go against the prevailing thought of his era and work to integrate his dream life into his waking life and work, as many today are now doing.

Dreaming in Early America

The Quakers of colonial and Revolutionary America used dreams to express their faith and even to bring about social and cultural change. Quakers saw dreams as night journeys that could be very powerful experiences and as a means through which God could communicate with humans.[10] The Quakers were a minor religious group compared with Anglicans,

9. For more information on Swedenborg, see the website of the Swedenborg Foundation, http://www.swedenborg.com/.

10. Gerona, *Night Journeys*, 2.

Methodists, Presbyterians, Baptists, and other Protestant groups that were also involved in settling the American colonies. Their well-documented use of dreams provided them with a way to reinforce their uniqueness, as well as to experience God or God's spirit in their lives. Mary Penington of England recorded this dream in 1644:

> I dreamed that night that I saw a book of hieroglyphics of religion, of things to come in the church or a religious state. I thought I took no delight in them, nor felt any closing in my mind with them, though magnified by those that showed them. I turned from them greatly oppressed, and it being evening, went out from the company into a field, sorrowing and lifting my eyes to heaven, cried: "Lord, suffer me no more to fall in with any wrong way, but show me the truth." Immediately, I thought the sky opened, and a bright light, like fire, fell upon my hand, which so frightened me that I awoke, and cried so that my daughter's servant, who was in the room, not gone to bed, came to my bed-side to know what was the matter with me.[11]

This dream narrative reflects the dreamer's desire for true faith. In this respect, it is like many dreams down through history, beginning in the Bible with the dreams of Jacob and Solomon and the visions given to Paul and Peter and continuing with the dreams of Constantine, St. Francis, and others. Dreams have been one of the ways God has turned people to faith or helped them purify or reform their faith. This function of dreams was helpful to Quakers as they moved from the fringes of society to the more genteel levels of their communities. The Quakers were greatly influential in the founding and development of the colony that became the state of Pennsylvania. In fact, dreams sometimes influenced Quakers to go into the mission field. Gerona describes one such case:

> James Dickinson was like many other missionaries who followed his dream to America. Like most, he had visionary experiences early. While still a youth in 1678, he had a vivid dream. In the powerfully dramatic vision, he saw an evil man trying to drive a sheep into the water. Dickinson tried to help the animal, but the man escaped to a bridge and threw the sheep down. Then a good man saved the sheep from drowning, took it to pasture, and defeated the evil person on the bridge. The allusions to Jesus and the devil would not have been lost on anyone who heard the dream.

---

11. Quoted in ibid., 36–37.

Dickinson looked to the dream to conquer his own battles with evil. He soon became a minister and continued to have visions.[12]

Of particular interest is the use of dreams in groups, which took place in some Quaker gatherings. When there was a desire to bring about a change in a particular faith community, some of the leaders or ministers might bring a dream to a group meeting. This is a different purpose for dream work than I'm suggesting for contemporary churches, but nonetheless, it is a precedent for using dreams in group settings for religious purposes. There is also evidence of dreams being interpreted differently by people on different sides of an issue or with different religious perspectives.

Dream work also helped Quakers strengthen their identity in the face of pressure from outside. As Gerona notes, "Indeed, Quaker dreamwork had primed individuals to have just the kind of evangelical rebirth that the Great Awakening depended on, and more than ever dreamwork became an essential component of Quaker ministry."[13]

Quakers used their dreams for a variety of purposes besides engendering faith in unbelievers or renewing faith in believers who had become lax or dispirited in their faith. As Quaker ministers traveled back and forth between England and America, they used their dreams to help influence their audiences. Young people were converted to Quakerism, often through the sharing of ministers' dreams or by the ministers' interpretations of the dreams of the young people. Dreams were also used to reinforce the new faith in young people, turning them against their parents and teachers.

Quakers were in the forefront of social movements for change in the eighteenth and nineteenth centuries. Their dreams reflect their concerns and indicate some of the dynamics of those issues. The area of social change that was most volatile for America in that period was that of race relations, specifically the issue of slavery. The following is Gerona's description of a dream of Elizabeth Webb, based on Webb's memoir of 1697:

> She dreamed that she "was a servant in a Great house," and while she was standing at a well, she "heard a voice which bid me go and call others to help me to Draw water." She approached a group of people in a chariot and recognized them as the servants she was sent to call. She saw that "they were both white and black people" and asked them, "Why have ye stayed so long [?]" They responded that "the buckets were frozen (and) we could come no Sooner."

12. Ibid., 93.
13. Ibid., 127.

The symbolic meaning of the dream is clear. The big house was the home of the elect, and God had called on Webb to preach to everyone. The frozen buckets of water represented their previous ignorance of Christianity. Webb concluded that "by the vision I was Satisfied that the Call of God was to the black people as well as the white." Although she had been initially unsure whether Africans should be Christianized, the dream convinced her of "the Universal Love of God to mankind.[14]

Another area of social relations in which Quakers have long been involved is that of peace and the nonviolent resolution of conflicts. John Woolman was a leading eighteenth-century Quaker, influential in the role Quakers played in the colony of Pennsylvania in particular. Here is a report of one of his dreams.

> John Woolman was another reform-minded minister who, among other things, urged Quakers to avoid wars and befriend Indians. In 1754 Woolman dreamed that as he stood in his orchard, two dull suns preceded a fiery storm. He told an acquaintance that he must be "resigned" to die because this fate awaited everyone. Then Woolman walked into a poorly built home containing many sad people. When he looked out the window, he saw three red streams and many ancillary ones flowing from earth to sky. A large army came down and taunted him, but he made no reply. Then a captain of the militia said that "these men were assembled to improve in the discipline of war." This dream was about creating a larger peace, not just between Quaker meetings but between British Americans and Native Americans.[15]

This was not the universal attitude of Quakers in the American Revolutionary period. According to Gerona, "The extreme pacifists were the most prolific dreamers (at least on record), skillfully weaving dream interpretations into allegorical stories to influence the community. Perhaps more than any other individual, prolific dreamer and writer Ann Emlen turned to her dreams to come to terms with Quaker divisions and justify her behavior.[16] The early American Quakers were contentious and disunited in this period, as seems to be the case with every religious group trying to establish its identity. What makes the Quakers of colonial and Revolutionary America unique is their use of dreams in their everyday religious life.

14. Ibid., 89. Capitalization is from the original.

15. Ibid., 148–49.

16. Ibid., 192.

One of the ways Quakers resisted the push towards war was through boycotts, a method still in use today.

> Pacifists, it turns out, engaged in the same traditions of radical protest, for example, the boycott, that Revolutionaries had employed effectively against England. . . . If Quakers were not known for their crowd actions, they nonetheless engaged in a rich tradition of radical protest—and this often turned on a dream.

Such actions as these are the roots of Quaker work that continues today in the areas of peace and reconciliation and racial harmony.

Another area of Quaker influence is their plain manner of dress and their desire for simplicity in life. Gerona quotes from a long, printed dream narrative from the early nineteenth century that touches on this subject of dress: "his raiment somewhat of sheepskin or bright fawn colour"; "a luster reflected from the light, which extended as the skirts of their garments, which appeared like a plain robe or covering"; "a number of persons, richly dressed, passed us, who smelled so strong of brimstone, that I seemed almost suffocated"; and "a fine person, very white or powdered, and richly dressed . . . and from her eyelids came small flashes of fire." Gerona states, "The message of this dream was clear to Quaker interpreters: simplicity was good, and ostentation was not. The people doomed to hell were those who were richly dressed and loved money."[17]

Quakers, like other people in the American colonies and during the post-Revolutionary War period, faced a variety of social upheavals related to issues such as the rights of women, economic change, and the relationship between the colonists and the British Empire. Dreams played a role in the way many Quakers met those challenges. Gerona notes: "Dreamwork thus continued to be one of the most creative aspects of Quaker religiosity as the American Revolution challenged the coherence of the British Empire,"[18] adding, "And despite the rise of deism and rationalism, dream stories spread like wildfire during the early 1800s. In fact, the biggest change following the war seems to have been the multiplication of people who turned to dreams to better understand themselves and their world."[19]

The dream narratives of Quakers in colonial and Revolutionary America reflect a period not all that long ago when dreams were a familiar part of the religious lives of believers. There are great differences between

17. Ibid., 160–63.

18. Ibid., 175.

19. Ibid., 206.

the way colonial Quakers used their dreams and the way I'm suggesting dreams be used. The nature of dreams has not changed, though—the only difference is the attitudes taken toward dreams and the way dreams are understood and interpreted and then put to use.

In the early days of the American colonies, most people held attitudes much in common with those prevalent in England, where most white colonial Americans had emigrated from. As Gerona points out, considerably more attention was paid to dreams in earlier periods of history than many people realize. As today's scholars and the modern dream movement look more closely at the role of dreams in human history, I would not be surprised to find a consistent use of dreams throughout the church at the level of popular practice. I cannot prove this contention, but it is my sense based on my years of research on this topic. What other times and places have seen a thriving interest in and use of dreams? Morton Kelsey, in *God, Dreams, and Revelation,* addressing the period between Pope Gregory I and the twentieth century, mentions great scholars and saints like Aquinas, Francis of Assisi, and John Calvin, as well as lesser-known theologians like Caspar Peucer and Jeremy Taylor (the seventeenth-century Anglican, not the twenty-first-century dream researcher). But, as in the case of the Quakers discussed above, how many times and places in the history of the Christian church has a popular involvement with dreams among ordinary people of faith been overlooked? Kelsey makes this comment about his research: "Leads about the church's thinking [on dreams] have turned up in scholarly works on Chaucer and on ancient Greece, in one of Jung's careful footnotes, in fact almost anywhere but in writings about the church."[20]

My sense is that interest in dreams has accompanied human development and church history since the days of the early church, but in our particular cultural and intellectual context we have not paid much attention to dreams. This brief historical survey barely scratches the surface. I am willing to bet that, as in the case of the dream narratives of Quakers that Gerona compiled, interest in dreams has been present throughout the history of the Christian church. Interest in dreams will most likely be found on the margins of the big theological issues of the times, but it will be there. Much remains to be uncovered in terms of how dream work has contributed to the life of the Christian church over the centuries.

---

20. Kelsey, *God, Dreams, and Revelation,* 145.

7

Dreams and Spirituality

Deeply disturbing is the failure of *rational people,* who can see
neither the chasm of evil nor the chasm of the holy, who with the
best of intentions believe that with a little reason they can reunify a
structure that is falling apart. In their lack of vision they want to do
justice to both sides and are thus caught in the crossfire between
clashing powers, without having accomplished the least bit.

—Dietrich Bonhoeffer, *Ethics*

The above quote from Dietrich Bonhoeffer is not a dream narrative, nor
was he writing about dreams. But Bonhoeffer's insights about the limits
of rationality fit the premise of this book in that dreams help us bridge
the chasm between the evil and the holy. Dreams may indeed portray the
depths of the evil in our hearts, just as they may portray the heights of our
spiritual communion. Paying attention to our dreams can give us insights
into our waking life, allowing us to see alternate possibilities that our life
holds. This is also one of the benefits of a life of prayer.

The issue of rationality is the main focus of this chapter. Dietrich
Bonhoeffer was a German pastor who was martyred by the Nazis just days
before his prison camp was liberated by the Allied forces. Bonhoeffer, more
perceptively than many other writers of his time, wrote about the challenges presented to the Christian church by the rise of National Socialism
in Germany. One of the popular arguments against rationalism I heard
years ago, but never verified, is that there were more PhDs in Germany at
the time the Nazis came to power than in any other country at that time.

That seems to reflect Bonhoeffer's sentiments in the above quote. How did something so evil arise among so many educated, rational people? I believe that one part of the answer is the unconscious forces that are operating in the world and in our souls, and I argue that the use of dreams in our prayer or spiritual lives will help us understand this better. Dream work does not repudiate rationalism; it simply gives us another form of information as we face the challenges of life.

The connection between dreams and spirituality is clear. The last generation or two of American mainline Protestant Christians have participated in a renaissance of prayer and devotional practices drawn from previous periods of Christianity. Much of the interest in Christian spirituality comes from the desire for more concrete experiences of God, more experiences of faith, not just doctrine or intellectual discourse about faith. One of my favorite statements on this subject is by Karl Rahner, who said, "The devout Christian of the future will either be a 'mystic', one who has 'experienced' something, or he will cease to be anything at all."[1] The contemporary believer needs something concrete to hang on to, not just an intellectual faith that is in accord with certain principles or dogmas. This desire for such experiences, for a more deeply rooted life of faith, has led to the growing appeal of spiritual practices. My premise is that dreams provide a readily and universally available means of experiencing the world of spirit, providing a transition into the kinds of experiences described in religious literature the world over—the mysticism Rahner is referring to. As I've already discussed, the use of dreams in the lives of Christians has not been widespread, but dreams do offer a way to experience life in the spirit.

In the introduction, I described my personal odyssey of faith. This chapter offers a deeper exploration of the specific practices that I've adopted in my personal spiritual quest over the past three decades. I will compare these experiences to my use of dreams in my spiritual quest. I hope readers will find parallels in their own searches for authentic spiritual practices. I propose that our dreams offer us daily access to the world of spirit and that our dreams counter the stranglehold that rationality has on our culture.

Introduction to Prayer

When I went to seminary in the mid-1970s, I was seeking a solid grounding in the Bible and Christian history for my faith. At one point I stumbled upon

1. Rahner, *Theological Investigations*, 7:15.

a book by John B. Coburn called *Prayer and Personal Religion* that featured five "foundation stones of prayer." These five suggestions became the pattern for my prayer life, a pattern that has lasted all the years since then. It's a basic routine consisting of prayers of adoration, thanksgiving, confession, intercession, and petition, which were standard forms of liturgical prayer that I'd used in Sunday worship since my youth. But these forms of prayer, which I'd associated with public worship and thus as reserved for Sunday mornings, felt strange as I began to use them in my daily personal prayers. It was something new for me.

A powerful breakthrough in my personal prayer language occurred when I began to practice Coburn's recommended prayer of adoration. The entire prayer is the simple phrase "God, I love you." This was not the way I had learned to pray, nor was it the way I'd learned I could address God. I was not raised with much emotional expression in my family, and to say "I love you" to anyone felt to me like a risky emotional investment. To speak that way to God was a real struggle for me as I worked to adopt Coburn's suggested method. But I persevered and later became quite comfortable with expressing my love to God. This opened me up to new depths of personal prayer and prayer language. Beyond this new level of intimate speaking to God, I also adapted the five methods of prayer recommended by Coburn to my dream work, which resulted in the basic pattern of prayer that has become my life-long practice.

Praying the Psalms

Yes, your Word is a lamp to my feet
and a light to my path
You give me strength as I descend into
 The inner sanctum,
To uncover the truth hidden there,
to seek the treasures of the Spirit.[2]

These verses from Psalm 119 reflect the encouragement and inspiration that Scripture can give to those seeking wisdom. The psalms have long offered encouragement and inspiration to Christians. Soon after I finished seminary, I expanded my personal prayer life by reading from the book of

2. Merrill, *Psalms for Praying*, 260–61.

Psalms on a daily basis. After I'd been in my first pastorate for about five years, I decided to put together a sermon series on the book of Psalms in the Old Testament. I discovered that *The Book of Common Prayer* of the Episcopal Church contains a psalter that assigns all of the psalms to morning and evening readings. Using this psalter, one could pray through the psalms over a thirty-day period. I began praying the psalms every morning and evening, according to this pattern.

Praying the psalms opened up another new depth of spirituality to me. As I read the psalms of lament and encountered the cries for vengeance in them, I was disturbed. These cries for vengeance did not seem to fit with the Christian faith where Jesus' words from the cross played a major role— "Father, forgive them, for they know not what they do" (Luke 23:34). How could I pray verses such as these?

> Let his days be few
>> and let another take his office.
>
> Let his children be fatherless,
>> and his wife become a widow. (Ps 109:7–8, *Book of Common Prayer*)

I struggled with the psalms' portrayal of such stark vengeance, and I studied the psalms to see what the church had said through the ages about these raw emotions. I learned again that the Bible takes human nature seriously and allows for the expression of the deepest emotions. In the case of these psalms of vengeance and lament, nowhere does the Bible encourage the person praying to actually carry out the vengeance their heart desires. Instead, the person praying asks God to carry out the vengeance. As I wrestled with these feelings and contrasted them to Jesus' words on the cross, I came to a better understanding of the place of deep emotions in the life of faith. This was helpful when I taught classes on the psalms, since I always had to lead the class through this process of understanding the deep emotions in the lament psalms.

This excerpt from one of my dreams portrays the depth of emotion referred to in the psalms of lament:

> *I walk into a garage. There is a guy lying on the ground, and when I approach him he throws a nail ball and hits me in the neck. The ball is about the size of a softball, so it also hits my shoulder and lower jaw. It sticks there for a minute, until I grab it and pull it off. It doesn't hurt and I see no blood, but I'm very affected by the*

malevolence implied in the act. I go lean over the guy and realize he
is in some kind of pain or anguish. I tell him he is going to die.

As I discuss in more detail in chapter 8, dreams will not always speak nicely, but they will speak honestly. The problem many people have with the psalms of lament is that these psalms speak so honestly. This dream spoke honestly about my feelings of anger at the dream character on the ground. When I did the dream work, I recognized that my anger was in response to what someone had done to me in the week or so before the dream. My spiritual practice of praying the psalms was, and continues to be, an aid in recognizing my true emotions. As I learned to pray the psalms, I continued to work on my dreams and find connections and common experiences between dreams and my praying the psalms. Sometimes this involved the synchronicity of having dreamt some particular action or emotion, then reading about that same action or emotion in that morning's reading of the psalms.

My practice of praying the psalms deepened as I learned about worship in Benedictine monasteries. My first two spiritual directors were both Benedictine monks, and when I visited them I often attended their monastery's worship services. Benedictine worship incorporates the psalms to such an extent that they pray their way through the entire psalter in one week. Their method is to chant the psalms in their services, using simple Gregorian chants taken from a variety of historical sources or written by contemporary composers. The singing of the psalms in Benedictine worship led to the deepening of my use of the psalms. The act of singing can more powerfully express our prayer and devotion. A popular expression is "Those who sing pray twice," which refers to the increased depth of our prayer when we sing our prayers instead of just speaking or reading them.[3] That was what I experienced in singing the psalms in Benedictine worship.

Lectio Divina

The spiritual practice of lectio divina was developed in the Christian church beginning around the third century, and it involves reading the Bible to hear God's word directly to the believer. This is different from what many Christians term as Bible study, a more intellectual and detached way of reading or using the Bible. Lectio divina seeks a personal application of a

---

3. The phrase "He who sings prays twice" is found in paragraph 1156 of the Catechism of the Catholic Church.

particular scriptural passage to oneself at the particular time in life when the practice is being performed. Lectio divina has played an important part in my developing practice of prayer and in my approach to dream work.[4] The element of lectio divina that can help in dream work is the method of focusing on all the elements of the particular Bible passage being used for the exercise of lectio. As we focus on the different elements of the Bible text selected for lectio, we expand our view of the situation, noticing little details that were not evident in prior readings of the text. In the same way, we can broaden our exploration of a dream by looking at the deeper meanings of images and actions in the dream, particularly as those images and actions are found in other areas such as culture, religion, mythology, and politics.

Also, through the practice of lectio divina we can gain deeper insight by using other senses, such as touch, smell, or sound, as we meditate on the biblical text, phrase, or word. Some of this aspect of lectio is projection, bringing the values and associations of our culture and conditioning to a text or word that may have had very different connotations in its original setting. In some approaches to Bible study, this would not be acceptable, but in the devotional practice of lectio, it is another way to approach the text or Word to see what God is saying to us today. In the same way, our dream work can benefit from our looking around the edges of a dream, re-calling the sounds, smells, or any other sensory experiences in the dream.[5] Dreaming is primarily a visual experience, but occasionally sounds or smells are involved in a dream, and it is helpful to notice them.

The Labyrinth

The labyrinth is an ancient practice that has recently grown in popularity after its "rediscovery" within the last couple of decades. This rediscovery can be attributed to one woman, the Rev. Dr. Lauren Artress, an Episcopal priest and psychotherapist who was formerly on the staff of Grace Cathedral in San Francisco. Artress has opened up the labyrinth as an ancient tool that helps modern people discover their spiritual depths. Her work with the labyrinths at Grace Cathedral is based on her experiences with the

---

4. See the brief introduction to my use of lectio divina in the introduction to this book.

5. Ignatius of Loyola uses an application of the senses in his Spiritual Exercises, particularly in Week 2, Day 1, Fifth Contemplation, which is an application of the five senses. Ignatius of Loyola, *The Spiritual Exercises*.

labyrinth at Chartres Cathedral in France.[6] It is important to know that a labyrinth is not a maze, though the terms continue to be used interchangeably. Labyrinths are designed to have one path into the center and one path back out. There are no blind passages, no dead ends, and no attempts to trick the walker. Mazes, on the other hand, are designed specifically to fool the person who enters them, as though they were riddles to be solved.

As I learned more about walking labyrinths, I discovered how well the practice suits my personality, particularly the fidgety energy in me. Many of us find sitting still for prayer or meditation a difficult thing to do. We are used to a fast-paced life, so slowing down and sitting still for prayer is difficult. It is worth the effort to try to sit still, but a labyrinth offers the opportunity to pray while we walk, a kind of halfway point between busy, active life and contemplative life. The activity of walking helps siphon off some of the excess psychic energy in our minds that can get in the way of our meditation or prayer. Many people find their best prayer times to be early morning or evening walks with their pets. You may find that you are most open to prayer and to listening to God and the world around you while you are out for a walk in your neighborhood or perhaps in hills or forests near where you live.

Walking a labyrinth has some of the same devotional qualities, but walking on a labyrinth serve as a better metaphor for life than a regular walk through the neighborhood or the woods. Turning in every direction several times, facing all directions of the compass, can remind us of all the aspects of our life, the various directions in which we have interests or concerns. Our specific intention to speak with God, or the Holy Spirit, or whoever or whatever we desire to speak with in our prayer, makes the labyrinth a more energetically charged environment.

We may find when we walk, either in nature or on a labyrinth, that the dominance of our rational mind is lessened, the part of us that manages our life, schedules all our activities, and thinks about what we are doing and where we are going. This rational thinking can be set aside while walking (again, either on a labyrinth or in nature), and thus we are better able to let our imagination take over. It is often in our imagination that God speaks to us. All these factors together have made walking the labyrinth a growing spiritual practice among people of all faiths, not just Christians. I myself became so enamored with walking labyrinths that I eventually took the

6. See Artress, *Walking a Sacred Path*. Chapter 3 discusses the various shapes of labyrinths and their history.

training offered by the organization that Artress works with, and some of my ministry now involves presenting labyrinth programs.

I have found that I am able to work my own dreams while walking a labyrinth. Here is part of a dream narrative that I took into the labyrinth at Grace Cathedral in San Francisco during my training to become a labyrinth facilitator.

> *I'm at a large family party in a place that seems like the house I grew up in. There are several children around who seem like my children and my grandchildren, but they are all about the same age. I get really angry with the kids, who are running all around and just generally being very rude.*

I worked this dream there on the labyrinth walk and found that I gained as much insight about the dream by simply walking and praying it in the labyrinth as I had through working with other dreams in dream groups. That experience has deepened my appreciation of the labyrinth. I had been recording my own dreams for nearly thirty years by the time I took the training in the labyrinth, so there was a natural desire for me to put the two together. Dreams and labyrinth walks both offer tools for our spiritual growth, and each may be complemented by the use of the other as we seek to experience a deeper spiritual life.

Praying with Icons

> *Then the scene changes into what I can only describe as a kind of slide show of faces of different people who all turn golden, glowing brighter and brighter. They are able to pass this glowing effect on to others, and the scene moves from one person to another, all glowing brighter and passing it on. There are men and women, young people and old people, standing or sitting. At first, they are all a deep golden yellow, and then they grow brighter and brighter until they are almost white before the next image appears.*

This was the conclusion to a powerful dream that woke me up, stunned with wonder as I reflected on the beauty and goodness of the closing scene. One of my first associations with this scene was the rich golden color that is often found in Orthodox icon paintings. It was as though the images of the people became icons themselves, objects used for prayer.

Praying with icons refers to a spiritual practice that uses icons from the Orthodox Christian tradition as tools in prayer. These icons are paintings of holy figures that follow a particular style and method of composition revered in Orthodox Christianity. Guided by Henri Nouwen's book *Behold the Beauty of the Lord: Praying with Icons*, I use specific icons in my daily prayers. Nouwen's book is very helpful because it is assembled in such a way that you can have the book open to a photo of a specific icon as you read his description and discussion of the image. Some people, particularly those in the Protestant tradition, have to overcome some resistance in order to learn to pray with icons. As a Presbyterian pastor, I was trained in the roots of the Protestant Reformation, which began in the sixteenth century. One of the minor points of the Reformation was the rejection of graven images and idolatry. Some of this was prompted by interchanges between Western European Christians and Eastern European Christians, the latter belonging to the Orthodox family of Christians.

John Calvin is the spiritual patriarch of the Reformed family of Christians, of which Presbyterians are a part. He strongly criticizes the use of icons by the Greek Orthodox Church:

> Thus is the foolish scruple of the Greek Christians refuted. For they consider that they have acquitted themselves beautifully if they do not make sculptures of God, while they wantonly indulge in pictures more than any other nation. But the Lord forbids not only that a likeness be erected to him by a maker of statues but that one be fashioned by any craftsman whatever, because he is thus represented falsely and with an insult to his majesty.[7]

Given my background as a Presbyterian pastor, it took some work on my part to appreciate the use of icons as a prayer practice. The difference between the culture that Calvin lived in and ours is immense. We are a visually dominated culture. Calvin's culture was much more focused on words, on preaching and on hearing the Bible. There were no such things as movies, television, computer screens, or the Internet that so dominate the lives of the average person today. A prayer practice that focuses on our sense of sight is appropriate for our culture and our time. Icons provide one way to compete with the images that surround us. Here are some insightful words from Nouwen:

> We need to be aware of the vast array of visual stimuli all around us. The "powers & principalities" are all around us attempting to control our daily images. Posters, billboards, TV, movies. . . . Still we do not have to be passive victims of a world that wants

7. Calvin, *Institutes of the Christian Religion*, 1.11.4.

to entertain and distract us. We can make some decisions and choices. A spiritual life in the midst of our energy-draining society requires us to take conscious steps to safeguard that inner space where we can keep our eyes fixed on the beauty of the Lord.[8]

The practice of praying with icons is another ancient prayer and devotional practice that can speak powerfully to us today because it is well suited to the contemporary preoccupation with visual stimuli and visual learning.

The connection between dreams and icon praying is that dreams offer us images of our own life that can be used as prayer foci. This occurs when using the method of dream work promoted in this book ("If it were my dream . . .") to work with icons. Examining one's personal responses to an icon can produce powerful insights into one's life and into the way God works. Examining one's personal responses to one's dreams can produce the same effect. Dreams and icons both share a focus on images. This is an area where building bridges between the two practices of praying with icons and using dreams in prayer life can benefit people of faith.

The difference between icons and dreams is their authorship. Icons are the product of a specific artist, or perhaps a school of artists, following particular rules that have been laid down over centuries.[9] Dreams, on the other hand come from . . . where? I like the phrase "the author of dreams" because it implies some kind of agency without requiring agreement about where dreams come from. Dreams use a common language and seem to have a set of rules of their own that are not laid down by humans, unlike the rules for painting icons. But there is a similarity in the way one looks at the images of dreams and icons to get to a deeper meaning for one's life and in one's prayers.

Spiritual Direction

Aside from working and praying with my dreams, the most important spiritual practice that I have adopted is spiritual direction.[10] Spiritual direction is another practice with long and deep roots in the history of the Christian church, beginning in the earliest days of the church and continuing through

8. Nouwen, *Behold the Beauty of the Lord,* 12.

9. Forest, *Praying with Icons,* 3-26.

10. Though spiritual direction as a practice pre-dates some of the other practices referenced in this chapter, I've left it until last. I spent over ten years meeting with spiritual directors before I decided to take the training to become a spiritual director myself.

the centuries. Spiritual direction is usually done on a one-to-one basis, with a trained director working with a directee. The director accompanies the directee in his or her life of faith, their walk with God. This practice has seen a resurgence in Protestant churches over the last couple of generations.

I had read about spiritual direction for years before I decided to seek my own director. This happened after I heard Rev. Eugene Peterson speak at a retreat on the topic of the care of pastors.[11] He offered several suggestions, but his entire presentation seemed to lead up to his strong endorsement of the benefits of spiritual direction. I approached Peterson during one of the breaks in the retreat and asked how to go about engaging a director to work with me. Within a few months I was involved in my first spiritual direction relationship with a Benedictine monk. That relationship lasted several years until the monk left the country to study abroad. Then I engaged another director, also a Benedictine monk.

After five years of being in a direction relationship with my second spiritual director, he died. I was grieving for a year or so and went without a director until a spiritual crisis prompted by the outbreak of the Iraq War of 2003 drove me to search for a new director. I have been in this, my third direction relationship, for over twelve years now, and it has been by far the richest of the spiritual direction relationships I have had. It is only in this third spiritual direction relationship that I have used my dream work. My current spiritual director is comfortable with dreams, and she has no difficulty with my bringing dreams into our conversations. This was not the case with my two previous directors. Whenever dreams were mentioned, their response was one of casual interest or curiosity, but dreams never became the focus of a direction session, as they may now.

Because of my appreciation of the benefits of spiritual direction in my own life, I took training to become a spiritual director myself and have been practicing as such for over eight years now. Some of my clients in spiritual direction come to me specifically because of my work with dreams.

I'm on a weekend trip with people I don't know, but they are members and faculty of the spiritual direction training program I'm enrolled in. I wind up with ["fall into," my notes say] a problem couple or family that includes a young man who is really hurt and angry. I do spiritual direction with him and then group spiritual direction with them all, in which I use a Darth Vader toy mask, the black plastic

11. The study book for this retreat was Peterson's *Working the Angles*. I found this book to be a very helpful guide for busy pastors who need to pay attention to their spiritual life.

one like my ten-year-old son has, as a kind of "talking stick" that
allows one person to talk while the others listen. The hurt guy gets all
his anger out and calms way down, then comes and leans his head
on my shoulder. They all bid me farewell with love and gratitude. I
feel I have really achieved something good here.

This dream gave me great insights into the role of spiritual direction
in my life. Not only did it reflect my work as a spiritual director, but I took
the dream to my own spiritual director for help with it. On the surface, the
dream portrayed me as a skilled director, addressing the needs presented
to me in such a way that the people involved were very grateful for what I'd
done. It thus fulfilled my fantasies and desires for my involvement in the
spiritual direction training program I was enrolled in. I liked these feelings,
but I wanted to know more about the dream. As my spiritual director and I
worked with the dream, I realized that the angry man could also represent
me and my anger at the various things that I've experienced in life. In addition, my spiritual director helped me see that feelings of being appreciated
can have both positive and negative effects. There is always a need for positive self-esteem, which is an important aspect of human life. But too much
self-esteem can get in the way of one's relations with others. This dream
provided material for good spiritual direction.

My training as a spiritual director has taught me that one of the tasks
of the spiritual director is to help the person seeking direction to notice
where God is present in his or her life. It is not a matter of creating a sense
of God's presence as much as noticing the sense of God's presence that is
already there. In working with our dreams, whether in a spiritual direction
relationship or not, the same pattern of noticing applies. Spiritual direction
can provide images that help the person in direction understand his or her
spiritual life at that time. Dreams provide a continual supply of images,
many of which are directly related to the dreamer's own life and experiences. By using the dream work methods included in this book, the spiritual
direction relationship can be enriched.

I believe dreams and our prayer life share many of the same experiences and
phenomena, and as we explore our life of prayer we can find many parallels in
our dreams and their effects upon us. This chapter has compared dream work
with some of the spiritual practices available today that I have had experience
with. I believe my spiritual experiences are similar to those of many people
who have explored new practices due to the re-emergence of spirituality in

the last few decades in America. I've described my experiences here because I know I'm not unique, not the only person seeking deeper spiritual experience. I've tried many popular spiritual practices over the decades, and nothing has fed me on a continual basis the way my dream work has.

Dreams are available to help sate the spiritual thirst that exists both inside and outside the Christian church. My audience is those inside the church, but much of what I propose here can be taken and used by anyone seeking a deeper spiritual life, a deeper meaning in their lives, and deeper connections to the world of spirit. Using our dreams can deepen and expand whatever spiritual practice or practices we may be involved in. Dreams provide universal and ready access to the realm of spirit. We all have dreams every night. The images, metaphors, and insights that come to us in our dreams enrich our spiritual lives. Dreams can help us identify our experiences of God, the mystical dimension of life. The key is learning how to use our dreams. I will explain how to do this in the next chapter.

8

The Value of Dreams

At the 2007 International Association for the Study of Dreams (IASD) conference, I was preparing to have lunch with a man who worked at a prestigious institute that researches spirituality and dreams and trains people to do dream work. I was anxious about what he would think about my work with dreams in the church. In thinking about the value of dreams for church people, I quickly came up with four points that seemed to me at the time the most obvious values of dream work. In the years since that lunch, I've found these four points to be of great value. Drawing on the metaphorical language of dreams, I refer to these as the four-legged dream chair.

The Four-Legged Dream Chair

A chair is one of the most universal pieces of furniture that humans use. Most cultures have chairs, which are pieces of furniture that people can sit upon to rest their legs and back. Chairs are used in gathering socially around a table or some other central focus. Chairs help us eat, relax, and even sleep. Chairs are basic to our lives. For me, the four-legged dream chair is a symbol of the four most important values dreams have in our lives. A chair can get by with three legs, but it is most stable with four legs. Of these four values of dreams, two are qualities of dreams that can be used by anyone and two are qualities that are particularly relevant for practicing Christians.

This four-legged classification system for the value of dreams has evolved for me over the years as I have watched and worked with my dreams and done the same with the dreams of other people. The four legs of the metaphoric dream chair are as follows: (1) dreams enhance our emotional self-awareness and honesty, (2) dreams help us set priorities in life, (3) dreams speak the language of prayer, and (4) dreams improve our biblical "literacy." I will look at each of these "chair legs" and give examples of dreams that illustrate the particular insight or principle at hand.

Dreams Enhance Our Emotional Self-Awareness and Honesty

> *I dream that I'm teaching Luke (my thirteen-year-old son) to drive an old Volkswagen in Big Sur, and I think about how terrible it would be to go off the side of one of the cliffs—it would surely kill us. There are no guard rails along the side of the road, and Luke is not very careful about staying away from the sides. He also reaches in between the spokes of the steering wheel to fiddle with stuff on the dashboard, and I have to tell him that's a dangerous thing to do. We wind up approaching a sharp turn in the road, and he is going too fast. I yell for him to slow down, but I think it's too late and we are probably going to go over the edge. Then I wake up.*

I was surprised by this dream; it told me I was concerned for my son and the world he was growing up into. At the time of this dream, I believed he was a fairly typical thirteen-year old, exploring his world and relatively oblivious to the dangers around him. He pushed the limits of his relationship with his parents yet was eager to learn from us. He was increasingly competent with computers and the Internet, and the evening before this dream I had noticed that on one of the screens he was viewing there was a link to a pornography site. I pointed that out to him and he moved on to something else. It wasn't until I recalled this dream and worked with it some the next morning that I realized how much that very brief experience the night before had affected me.

We humans have the propensity to lie to ourselves or to make little of emotions we don't want to face or feel awkward about. In the case of my dream experience above, I just didn't take the time in my waking life to look at my emotions. The dream reminded me that there were deeper issues at play in my experience with my son the night before.

Religion, culture, education, and family traditions all pressure us to feel that it is wrong to express or even feel certain basic human emotions. I think of the expression I heard growing up, "If you can't say something nice, don't say anything at all."[1] That may result in superficially smooth family or social relations, but it is not always good for mental health. Dreams will not always speak nicely, but they will speak honestly. That honesty may be disturbing or threatening, but I believe our dreams help us to look at those parts of our life that need further attention. Dreams call our attention to a particular aspect of our lives, and they do so in whatever way works best to get our attention. This may be expressed through repeated or recurring dreams. Should the situation be a serious one, we may have nightmares, dreams that disturb us greatly, as discussed in chapter 1. These kinds of dreams call attention to something in our life that needs resolution and do so in a way that screams more and more loudly until we address the issue.

Sometimes, even if a dream is not threatening, shocking, or socially unacceptable, we may not understand it but may still feel that it has something to tell us that we would like to know. When this happens, dream groups can be very helpful.

> My buddy Rick and I pull into a shopping center, where my favorite grocery store and my son's old taekwondo studio are located, to get some late-night food. It's very dark, so dark that we can just barely make out two areas with parked cars, each near a business that is open. One open place is a bar, but we are heading for a grill or coffee shop; I'm not sure which. As our lights shine on the area we are heading for, we notice a group of motorcycles parked together. Our headlights are very dim and just barely illuminate the bikes. We go into the coffee shop, which seems more like a bar or pizza place, with wooden picnic tables and sawdust on the floor. The bikers are there in leather vests, but they are clean-shaven weekend bikers. They are talking loudly and roughly, though, and I sense a more immediate threat from their attempts at proving themselves than from any actual evil intent. They are ordering mule steaks, and since I plan to order fish, I expect to be ridiculed.

Working with this dream on my own got me nowhere, yet I felt some strange attraction to it, some energy in it that I just didn't understand. When I have

---

1. When I mention to others that this phrase was part of my growing up in mid-twentieth-century America, I am met with almost universal agreement. When I use the phrase in public presentations, heads nod throughout the audience. As Sue Monk Kidd puts it: "When I was growing up, if my mother had told me once, she'd told me a thousand times, 'If you can't say something nice, don't say anything at all.' I'd heard this from nearly everybody. It was the kind of thing that got cross-stitched and hung in kitchens all over my native South." Kidd, *The Dance of the Dissident Daughter*, 8.

a dream like that, I like to take it to a dream group to see what others might find in my dream. Here is what the group came up with for this dream.

> My future was unclear to me, dim, and the dim light in the parking lot made it difficult to navigate. My buddy, Rick, has been something of a steady presence, an anchor for me. We had chosen this particular shopping center because it seemed safe, yet we ran into trouble even there. Life too can follow the same path. We can think we are heading into a safe and familiar place but encounter threats or problems nevertheless. I have different parts of my personality; the meat-eating part is loud, boisterous, and tries to impress others. There is also the part that is more modest, more withdrawn. Which of those parts of me do I give expression to? Where am I safe and where am I vulnerable? Is there a part of me that likes to be an outlaw on the weekends?

This dream occurred at a point in my life when I was contemplating a new direction for myself, one that would include more schooling and maybe some risk to my career. When the group was finished with my dream, I realized that the dream had spoken accurately and honestly to me about how I felt about the life change I was contemplating. This was a deeper and more satisfying understanding of the dream than I had been able to come up with by myself. I don't believe I would have come to these insights without the help of the dream group.

Another way to talk about the emotional honesty of dreams is to note that dreams are deep but not direct.[2] Dreams reveal the deepest parts of us, but they do it in ways that usually start out gentle and mild. If we are willing to work with our dreams, we may find resolution to the issue in our life the dream is trying to address. If we ignore the dream, we find we have recurring dreams that give us the same message. If we persist in ignoring the recurring dreams, the images in the dreams may become more and more frightening until the dream takes on the feelings of a nightmare. Deep parts of ourselves are revealed in our dreams. If we pay attention to and work with our dreams, they will reveal those deep parts of ourselves in a gentle, even playful way. In a dream group, dreamers can explore parts of themselves they may be uncomfortable with. Deep personal issues may be uncovered, and the group can be a wonderful small community of support, accompanying each dreamer through the exploration of their inner

---

2. The phrase "deep but not direct" was given to me by fellow IASD member Clare Johnson at a regional IASD conference in Lincoln, England, in September 2007.

life revealed in their dreams. Dreams are deep, but they are not direct in a confrontational way for most people. Here, the distinction needs to be made between dream work for personal growth and dream work for therapy or healing. Personal growth is what we do in many church and religious settings. We strive for a closer walk with God, for deeper spiritual and religious insights, perhaps for help with a decision in our life. Dreams can be wonderful tools in this area.

Healing or therapy is needed when religious, psychological, or emotional issues become so powerful and debilitating that we are unable to function well in our daily lives or our health is affected. Dream work may be used to explore the deeper elements in our lives, in our past and in our emotional development, in such a way as to bring us healing. This is an area of dream work that is best left to professionals— psychologists, psychiatrists, or social workers trained in emotional and psychological healing. If you are an individual working with your own dreams, the depth of your emotional response to a dream or image is one criterion by which you can determine whether you need professional help.

Dreams Help Us Set Priorities

I dream that I'm looking at the pledge cards that have come into the church and am surprised at the levels at which some families are contributing to the church. One couple in particular is among the bigger givers, but they never come to church. I think to myself that I really should make a home visit to them.

I had this dream in the fall of 1977, within a month of my ordination, when I was just beginning to serve as pastor of my first church. This was my first experience of a dream showing me something specific about my work as a pastor. It was also a very direct dream in that within the dream itself I thought that I should make a home visit. Most such prioritizing dreams are not quite that direct—the insights come later, as one reflects on the dream.

I call such dreams *prioritizing dreams* because they help me consider the priorities in my life and work. Our dreams remind us of things that might otherwise slip below the radar screen of our conscious lives. Dreams provide another avenue of information, another means of input into our lives. They help us see the larger picture of what's going on around us and widen our focus on life. In my career as a pastor I've used my dreams, particularly the small parts of my dreams that might otherwise be considered day residue, to help me provide pastoral care. They suggest particular church members I might want to call upon in their home, as in the above example. Perhaps I just need to make a phone call or send an email, or maybe I should consider this person or situation as a special focus for prayer. When something like this shows up in a dream, it helps me realize that something took place recently that I need to pay more attention to.

The term *day residue* in the previous paragraph refers to dreams that are related to events of the previous day. Contrary to the theory that most dreams are random firings of neurons in the brain while we are asleep,[3] I like to ask deeper questions of the particular day residue that I recall in my dreams. Why do I recall a dream about this particular part of the day and not another part? Is there something I need to know or observe or recall that a dream image of day residue is presenting? The benefits I've gained by using the day residue in my dreams as an additional source of information verify the value of working with this material. I noted above the first such dream that I had, within weeks of my ordination. But the experience of making priorities and decisions on the basis of my dreams has become commonplace for me in the thirty-plus years since then.

Likewise, if I casually see someone at church and then dream about them that night, I then examine my relationship with them, my interactions and history with them. Is there some reason to give them a phone call or stop by their house or send an email? Likewise, if the name of someone in the congregation is mentioned in a conversation and then I dream about them that night, it is always worth my while to do the same self-examination and see if there might be a reason to contact them. In this way, my dreams function as an extra source of intelligence and information, expanding the picture I have of my life and my work.

I once had the opportunity to speak to medical residents in a training program. I told them of my pastoral experiences and suggested that if they paid attention to their dreams they might be prompted to reconsider their work with particular patients. In parallel fashion to my experiences, if a doctor dreams of a patient he or she has seen recently, they might want to take another look at that patient's chart or the notes they have on that patient or, perhaps most importantly, to reflect upon their interactions with the patient that did not make it into their notes or patient chart. Our dreams often pick up on subtle, seemingly unimportant details. Has some

---

3. This theory is discussed in chapter 1.

new idea come to them, some avenue of exploration that had not occurred to them before?

A teacher had the following dream that illustrates this principle:

> *I dream I was in some sort of program and we were learning how to handle weapons. Someone was sitting high up on a ledge and was aiming his gun at me, and I raised my gun and shot and hit him right in the forehead. He looked really surprised and then fell over. I was very upset that I had killed him. I was telling my husband I thought we all had blanks. Enrique [one of my students] came over very excited and told me that if I had not gotten that person, think of how many others he might have shot.*

The teacher knew this dream was associated with her relationship with her student Enrique. When teachers dream of their students, what might their dreams tell them about the students, the teacher's feelings about the students, or the interactions between teacher and students? Though this dream is not what I would call a "teacher's nightmare," there is still information here that the teacher was able to apply to her relationship with this particular student, encouraging her to be more attentive to him and his opinions and insights.

This is an example of a nurse's nightmare:

> *I started a new job at an unfamiliar hospital. I got along well with my co-workers and was learning the floor routine and charting when I realized that the shift was almost over and I didn't know who my patients were and whether they needed treatments, IVs, or medications.*

Any job that includes responsibility for others or accountability to others will generate these kinds of dreams. They generally reflect the dreamer's fear at the time of the dream of being overwhelmed by the job. This sense of being overwhelmed is an aspect of the dream that gives the dreamer an honest picture of his or her emotions, as mentioned in the section above. In the nurse's dream, it is helpful to look at the word play between "patients" and "patience"; perhaps the dream is suggesting that the nurse should be patient with herself in her new job. Such dreams offer the dreamer clues that might be helpful in their lives at the time of the dream. The above examples relate to work as a pastor, physician, teacher, and nurse, but the ability of our dreams to provide an alternative source of information can apply to any person's life or occupation. The examples of so-called "dream discoveries" in chapter 1 reveal that this prioritizing can benefit not only the dreamer but also those around them, even on a global level.

I want to repeat here that I'm not willing to throw out the baby with the bath water by rejecting the scientific theories and models on which much of our modern industrial culture is built and returning to a primitive worldview, where we are haunted by unseen forces mediated through our dreams. My point is that our ability to learn from our dreams can provide an extra layer of information, beyond what science can yield, that aids us in our interactions with the world around us. This may particularly be the case for Christians who are trying to be faithful servants in the world. This leads to the third "leg" in my four-legged chair metaphor for dreams.

Dreams Speak the Language of Prayer

I'm on a boat that is either on a river or on a calm ocean. My mother, my wife, and others are there with me, and we are all fishing. My mother and wife have caught fish, but I haven't yet. My mother gives me her pole, which is long and thick in the handle area, and soon I begin to get hits on the fishing line. I look down in the water and can see large yellow and white shapes moving ten feet below the surface. I assume they are fish, and I hope to catch some.

I dreamt this the night after the opening of the first conference I ever attended of the International Association for the Study of Dreams (IASD), which was held in Berkeley, California, in June 2005. I was greatly disappointed in the evening program and went to bed praying my experience at the conference would improve. The above dream captured my desire to "catch" something from this conference. The dream itself expressed my desires, but it was my experiences at the conference the morning after the dream that made the dream more powerful.

I shared the dream with a group of people who were also new attenders of these conferences. The IASD conferences offer a wide variety of dream groups and morning exercises every year. This particular dream group was designed to be an entry into dream work at the conference and was aimed at people who were attending the conference for the first time. The group leaders opened the group by asking for responses to the program the night before. I registered my disappointment over the opening program with the group. Then two women shared their very positive responses to the program the evening before. Suddenly, my dream became more powerful and alive for me. The next phase of the group was actually sharing dreams that group members had the night before. I volunteered to share my dream because it had become so much more vivid for me after the group opening. The responses from the two women in the group enabled me to connect to the two women in my dream, even though in the dream they were clearly my mother and my wife. Whatever the identity of the women in the dream and their connection to me, they became pointers to me for how I might be more open to what was presented at the conference. In ways that I cannot scientifically explain, my prayer to get something out of this conference was answered. I noted the way the dream helped by conveniently coming on the first full day of the conference. This experience dramatically linked my dreams and my prayer life.

Synchronicity is sometimes a significant aspect of dreams. This is a dream recounted by a woman in a church dream group that was meeting for the first time.

> I'm walking through an upscale home that is very spacious. The home belongs to two friends of mine. They tell me they are willing to sell it to me for $410,000, but it has to be cash. I'm thinking to myself that $410,000 is a lot of money but not unreasonable for this house.

This dream was not that unusual, nor was it particularly powerful for the dreamer. In working with the dream, however, another woman in the group was astounded at the figure of $410,000 because she'd had two experiences in the previous ten days with that exact amount. These two women had not met until this day, the first gathering of the dream group. It was a very dramatic opening. This is how I responded to that experience when the group met the following month:

> My understanding has always been that God—or the Holy Spirit, the third person of the Trinity in the Christian understanding of God—has enabled such experiences to happen, and the more I try to live faithfully—the more I am "in tune" with the world—the more these "synchronous" events occur. So, our experience with the figure of $410,000 is an invitation from the Holy Spirit for us to be together in a good way, a way blessed by the Spirit. It is a nice opening, a nice invitation to us to spend this time together.

This was a dream group in a church, so the language of the Holy Spirit was not foreign to the group members, but they were surprised at the power of their personal experience. I will talk more about experiences of synchronicity, precognition, and other psi phenomena in chapter 10.

William Temple, a twentieth-century archbishop of Canterbury, is often quoted as having said, "When I pray, coincidences happen, and when I don't, they don't.[4]" Since I've had that experience myself, I feel this statement to be true. In recent years, I explored more deeply the Jungian concept of synchronicity as I'd experienced it in my dreams and spiritual life. Jung defines synchronicity as follows: "I mean by synchronicity . . . the not uncommonly observed 'coincidence' of subjective and objective happenings, which just cannot be explained causally, at least not in the present state of our knowledge."[5]

I believe Temple and Jung are talking about the same phenomenon. Dreams and prayers both lead to experiences of synchronicity. One of the ways that we Christians might become more comfortable with our dreams is to make this link with the life of prayer. Sometimes the experiences of synchronicity in a dream group can be startling, as in the example above of the figure of $410,000. For many people of faith who are accustomed to feeling that their prayers get answered in ways they cannot fully explain, the extra reinforcement and validation that synchronous experiences bring can be encouraging. It can also open the way for them to take more interest in their dreams. Or, as the popular saying goes, "A coincidence is God's way of remaining anonymous."

It is challenging to scientifically "prove" synchronicity or the effectiveness of prayer. Though some experiments seem to prove that prayer does have an effect on physical things, it is still not generally accepted scientifically that prayer "works." Yet for those of us in the faith community, prayer is a big part of our faith practice, regardless of scientific proof or verification. The faithful of all religions have been praying for centuries, and the experience and consequences of prayer keep us praying. The issue of synchronicity here in relation to dreams is another validation of the effectiveness of prayer.

For centuries, mainline churches (those churches that have been part of the power structure of the cultures and societies in which they find themselves) have adopted the rational worldview of Western civilization. When it comes to the ancient practice of prayer, the influence of this rational worldview has been to ask, "Does prayer change things?" The usual, if sometimes only implied, answer is, "No, but it changes the one praying." The issue of synchronicity or coincidence challenges this assumption—indeed,

4. Quoted in Watson, *Called and Committed*, 83.
5. Jung, *Collected Works: The Structure and Dynamics of the Psyche*, 8:205n118.

it challenges the dominance of the rational worldview. My aim is not to overturn that worldview and revert to what might be called a primitive worldview but to integrate the older, primitive worldview with the modern, rational worldview (in a sense, this is the Hegelian process of thesis, antithesis, and synthesis). I believe that combining modern psychological insights about dreams and dreaming with the respectful and serious approach that more ancient or primitive cultures have toward dreams can lead to a richer understanding of self as well as a richer spiritual life. Synchronicity experiences lead me to wonder how much prayer affects the world around us, if not outright changes it. Do experiences of synchronicity actually change things? I believe they change the dreamer or the one praying, in part by opening wider the possibility that such connections exist. Synchronicities can be accessed more readily through paying attention to one's dreams or through a regular discipline of prayer.

Related to this is the guidance or connection with life that both prayer and dream work provide in ways that cannot be rationally explained. I had always assumed that this guidance and/or connection was related to my life of prayer, but now I have an expanded understanding of dream work and realize that these experiences are also common for those who work with their dreams. I've had experiences that were so coincidental they seemed predestined. One of the most dramatic happened while I was in seminary, just a few years after beginning a regular prayer routine and starting to record my dreams in a journal.

I had flown from the San Francisco area to Utah to interview for a church job. On the flight back from Utah, my seatmate and I struck up a conversation. He had boarded at a previous stop. Within just a few minutes we discovered that we were both Presbyterians returning from interviews with prospective churches. He was already ordained and I was seeking my first call. The chances of such a meeting taking place are astronomically small. Was it mere coincidence or was there something else going on? Because I've had countless such synchronicities, I am no longer surprised by such events and now simply observe, "There's another one."

I have noticed over the years I've worked with dream groups that group members tend to experience an increase in synchronicities as they become more involved with their dreams and the dreams of others. They acknowledge that these events seem tied to their dream work. Beyond that, talking about their experiences related to their dreams has freed up group members to talk about such experiences in other parts of their lives. How do we account for such experiences? Within the Christian community we have the biblical precedent and the witness of the history of the Christian church, both of which say this is the action of the Holy Spirit of God. One of my favorite examples is the story in Acts 10 of Peter and Cornelius. Both men receive visions that lead to their coming together and having spiritual breakthroughs, signifying the opening up of the gospel to Gentiles. Reading the story, I notice that the visions sound dreamlike, and I wonder if Peter and Cornelius had taken naps in the afternoon when these visions took place. However one reads the story, it sounds like the same kind of coincidences or synchronicities that I am talking about here.

I've been involved in church retreats where things happen that are totally unplanned, yet they happen in such a way as to seem related but with no visible means of making the connection. These are programs in which the participants are much involved in prayer. I recall one retreat where a particular hymn was chosen by two leaders independently of each other for situations that were very much unrelated beyond occurring at the same retreat. Both people exclaimed, "We did not plan this!" I simply said to myself, "There's another one"—another synchronistic prayer-related experience. In situations of a highly charged nature like a retreat where everyone shares a common purpose, there are often occurrences of coincidence or synchronicity that affect the participants powerfully. Religious people will say something like "It's a God thing" to try to explain it. I believe that this kind of synchronicity is an action of God's Holy Spirit and that it is very much like what happens to those who pay attention to their dreams and share them with others.

Dreams Improve Our Biblical Literacy

I am wrestling with a seminary classmate in what seems like the back seat of a car or the rear end of a sport utility vehicle. I'm lying next to him, and we are both facing up. There is a large knife with a 12–14" blade that is lying in such a way as to be pointing at me and coming from him. It has a 3-D effect, like in 3-D movies.

This dream happened a few years after my graduation from seminary, when I and this classmate had gone our separate ways, but my work with the dream led to an association with another pastor at a nearby church with whom I was struggling at the time of the dream. My first association was that the knife was a threat to me, that this particular pastor meant to harm me and was perhaps threatening my new career as a pastor. But when I talked about the dream with a spiritual director, she pointed out Heb 4:12: "Indeed, the word of God is living and active, sharper than any two-edged sword, piercing until it divides soul from spirit, joints from marrow; it is able to judge the thoughts and intentions of the heart." When she asked me what positive image I might make of this knife/sword in my dream based on Heb 4:12, it came to me that God was challenging me through this dream to be able to "cut to the chase," to discern what my attitude and behavior needed to be in faith towards this other pastor and this situation. What had felt like a threat in the dream became a source of inspiration and help as I worked with the dream and carried it into my waking situation.

Dreams and religion speak the same language—the language of symbol and image. When we become more familiar with our dreams and the images and symbols they use, we broaden and deepen our reading and understanding of the Bible. I'm not referring only to the dreams described in the Bible, as discussed in chapter 5, though the application works there. The parables of Jesus, the metaphors and images of the prophetic books, the book of Revelation—all become more readily understandable when we become comfortable with the types of images and symbols that we find in the Bible as well as in our dreams. Think of the parable of the laborers in the vineyard in Matt 20:1–16. This parable angers or frustrates many people who hear it. In the story, an employer paid his laborers the same amount, no matter how many hours of the day each had worked. The parable goes against all ideas of fairness in the world of employment, but it provides a great example of God's grace being available to all, irrespective of their ability to earn it. If we were unfamiliar with the story or with the Christian Bible and had a dream like this, our reaction would be, "That was a strange dream!" Yet it is that very strangeness that begins to crack open our ability to hear something different from what we usually hear, breaking the grip of the rational or linear way of thinking promoted by Western culture.

One of the most popular and powerful parables is the parable of the prodigal son found in Luke 15. The depth of the father's ability to forgive his wayward son is startling. Throughout history, this parable has had a strong influence and has spilled over into our idiomatic language and way of thinking. Yet, if one were unfamiliar with the Bible and Western cultural history and were to dream such a story, our initial reaction would be, "Wasn't that a strange dream." Once we become accustomed to tending our dreams, we will find lots of little twists and unexpected turns of plot in the stories our dreams have told us during sleep.

My favorite example of dream images being helpful in Bible reading and study is the book of Revelation. This book is difficult for many Christians to understand. In fact, Martin Luther, the great Reformer and theologian of the sixteenth century, questioned why the book of Revelation was even included in the canon of Christian Scripture.[6] Because of the mysterious symbols and images it contains, the book of Revelation has had some of the wildest interpretations down through the centuries. A close analysis of this book shows that all its images and symbols come from what we know as the Old Testament and the Jewish apocryphal literature that immediately preceded the period of the New Testament. It's as if someone took a blender or food processor and put into it images and symbols from earlier Jewish literature, then turned the blender on for a moment and poured out the results, saying, "Look at all the new meanings we can get from this old material!"

This is much the same way that our dreams work. They take material from our past and current waking life and mix them up in such a way as to give us a new understanding of our current situation and of future possibilities.

> *I dream I am at a retirement party for my friends Ed and Ralph. Many people are gathered around them who know them and, through them, know me as well. Some of them give me small pieces of paper on which are written various things, but I don't read them. I look out a window of the building and see a group of people dancing in the parking area. They are people that I knew when I worked for Ed.*

Ed and Ralph are two men who served as mentors to me for several years at two different periods in my life. At the time of the dream, Ed was dead and Ralph was retired. This dream came to me at a point in my life when I was branching out into some new territory. I took inspiration from the dream because it felt like two parts of my past experiences and times of growth were coming together as I ventured into a new period of growth and study. In this new endeavor, I was using skills that I had learned when I worked

6. In the preface to his 1522 commentary on the book of Revelation, Luther writes, "I miss more than one thing in this book, and it makes me consider it to be neither apostolic nor prophetic." He adds, "I can in no way detect that the Holy Spirit produced it." Luther, *Luther's Works*, 35:398. Luther's view is somewhat more temperate in his preface to the 1546 commentary, but his relative disdain for the book of Revelation is still evident.

with Ed and Ralph. The dream told me I was integrating those skills to better serve those around me. This dream did not contain specific biblical images as the book of Revelation does, but it did use images from previous parts of my life to encourage me in this new venture, in the same way Revelation used images that were familiar to the early Christians. Dream language and biblical language have much in common, and dreams can help us in our faith lives as we work with the Bible.

The following dream is another illustration of the same process.

> *My wife and I are moving back into my old house in American Fork, Utah. I take her over to look out the window and show her the view of Mount Timpanogos. It is wider than in reality and has a few peaks that look like spires in several places. There is also a dusting of snow on the topmost parts. We pack up the car and get ready to drive up into the mountains for an outing. The car is parked in the back yard, which is mostly a cement pad. We have some trouble getting the car turned around and have to maneuver around some stuff. When we finally get out to the street I point out a large ice cream store that is on the corner of 700 North and 600 East and tell her that will mean trouble for us, as we will be eating ice cream more often than would be healthy for us. It is two stories tall, with a big advertisement for itself painted on a blue wall that faces 600 East. There are two or three other stores or shops on the corner too, quite different from when I lived there.*

This dream has some similarities to the power and images of my "Deeper American Fork House" dream that is discussed in the introduction to this book. It is set in the same location, and some of the same family connections are there. In both dreams there is a mix of former and current parts of my life. That mix provides insight for me, direction towards the integration of older parts of myself with current parts, and offers help in my becoming more of what and who I might be. Again, there are no specific biblical images here, although the mountain seen from the window could be an allusion to mountains in the Bible. But, the way this dream mixes past and present to give me a new view on the present is parallel to the way the book of Revelation uses the same dynamic to encourage its readers and listeners to view their lives in a new way. Learning to be comfortable with our dreams' dream language—the way dreams present different views of the present and the past, as well as possible futures—is a dynamic found often in Christian Scripture. This is a valuable form of biblical literacy.

Dreams may provide valuable sources of information to us that help us live our lives, whether we are religious or not. This chapter has explored four major insights into the use of dreams in our waking lives. Two of the insights into the value of dreams—enhancing our emotional honesty and helping us prioritize our life—are insights that anyone can use, whether they believe in a particular religion or not. The other two insights—using the language of prayer and improving our biblical literacy—are more specifically applicable to believers. The examples are specifically for Christians and Jews, who are Bible-based believers.[7] One of my hopes for this book and the position it takes towards working with dreams is to make a contribution towards wedding the scientific view with the historical religious view of dreams. My vision of this coming together of science and religion undergirds my attitude towards dreams and my work with dreams. If we pay attention to our dreams, they can give us a bigger picture of our life and offer us a valuable source of knowledge and wisdom. Dreams can be wonderful tools in developing and applying our faith. The next chapter will develop this theme further.

7. See Bar, *A Letter That Has Not Been Read.*

9

How to Work with Your Dreams

Time, like an ever rolling stream, soon bears us all away
We fly forgotten, as a dream dies at the opening day.

—Isaac Watts, "Our God, Our Help in Ages Past"

This chapter is designed to help you get started in the process of using your dreams in your prayer life. Perhaps you've been impressed with the role of dreams in the Bible or church history and you're interested in using your dreams to understand yourself better. Or perhaps you jumped right to this chapter and are ready to plunge in and use your dreams in your spiritual life. Either way, this chapter will give you what you need to get started. I will offer plenty of suggestions and options, and I encourage you to choose the ones that best fit you at this point in your life.

Write Dreams Out

The first step is to begin keeping track of your dreams. The hymn by Isaac Watts quoted above refers to how easily we forget our dreams. There are several ways to keep dreams from being forgotten, but they take some effort. Some dreams are so powerful and impressive that we may recall them for years to come, but the majority of our dreams die as the day opens before us unless we make an effort to recall them. Perhaps the most popular method for keeping track of dreams is to write them down. Other methods also work to recall and keep track of our dreams. Drawing or painting them may be the best method if you are artistically inclined. Or, speaking into a tape recorder or some other sound-recording device may work for you.

Whatever method you use, you need a record of the dream—the characters, actions, colors, emotions, etc., that you experienced in the dream. This may be cumbersome at first as you adapt yourself and your daily schedule to include this practice. I suggest you try a variety of methods for recording your dreams. You will develop a system that works well for you.

I write by hand in a small yellow tablet and transcribe the notes into my computer in greater detail later, after I've fully woken up and begun my day. Depending upon your sleeping arrangements, you may want to turn on the light next to your bed or get up and go to another area to make your notes. Some of this depends upon whether you sleep alone or with a partner. If your sleeping partner is a heavy sleeper, getting up or turning on lights may work. If your sleeping partner is a light sleeper, you will need a note-taking method that will not disturb them. I've tried several methods over the years. Ballpoint pens are available with a light in the tip that comes on when you press the button to engage the pen, but I've found they give too little light for my needs. In addition, the ink needs to flow downward in a pen, which can be a problem if you are lying on your back as you write your dream notes. I've found as I get older that if I come fully awake in writing my dream notes, I may not be able to get back to sleep, particularly if I've already had several hours of sleep. This becomes an issue when I have a full day's work ahead of me and need to get a good night's sleep. When I make my dream notes, I try to do so in a way that disrupts my return to sleep as little as possible. So, often I grab the notepad and my pencil and try to maintain whatever position I was sleeping in when I woke up.

I have settled on using a pencil for taking notes on my dreams. I attach a penlight to a pencil with a rubber band, making it relatively easy to grab the pencil, click on the light, write my notes in whatever position I'm lying in, put the notepad down, and go back to sleep. I try to do this without waking my wife, who is asleep next to me. Why a pencil? I read a joke several years ago in *Reader's Digest* magazine about the U.S. government spending $40,000 in an effort to develop a pen that would work in space, where there was no gravity to draw the ink out of the pen. Forty thousand dollars! The Russians wisely used a pencil, which does not depend upon gravity to make its marks. By using a pencil I can write in any position in bed, which helps me go back to sleep.

How extensive do the notes made during the night need to be? That depends upon your experience with recalling dreams. In the beginning, more extensive notes may be necessary, especially if the dream is not very intense. Sometimes a dream is so vivid and intense that just a word or two will recall the whole dream to you in all its vividness. I've found that over time my notes can be shorter and shorter and I can still recall enough of my dream to be useful. Because of my concern about getting back to sleep, I aim to minimize the note taking.

The method you use to keep track of your dreams over time depends upon your personal style. Many dreamers I know use journals, spiral-bound or specially bound books of blank pages. These necessitate handwritten notes and dream records. The advantage of this is that you can easily include sketches, collages, photos, or any other medium that might facilitate your dream recall and dream work. Leaving sufficient blank space around particularly powerful dreams that you put into your journal will enable you to add drawings, pictures, or more verbal commentary later. Some of our more spectacular or big dreams can stay with us for years, continually revealing new depth and insights. If you've left space around your original dream notes, you can add further insights, illustrations, or photos later.

A famous example of this kind of illustrated dream journal is Carl Jung's *Red Book*. The book is a large portfolio-type work containing pictures and drawings that Jung created over a period of fifteen years. It provides a model for how a personal journal can be used in an ongoing process over the years. A dream journal, in particular, can trace dreams or a series of dreams and help the dreamer reflect upon his or her growth based on one dream as that dream echoes in the dreamer's life. Or, a recurring image can be followed through other dreams or waking events.

Jeremy Taylor, author of several books on dreams, keeps a running series of such large journals. The last time I talked to him, he had created over ninety journals. Such dream journals will often contain reflections on life, on events in the world around the journal writer, etc. One of the interesting ways to use a journal is to document the synchronicities in your life. As I note elsewhere, synchronicities occur more often as you get involved with your dream life, and it can be helpful to document these experiences of synchronicity, precognition, etc. The documentation of these experiences is an extension of dream work. These experiences, combined with dream work, give the dreamer a larger picture of how the Holy Spirit is working in his or her life.

One of the ways I have expanded my journaling has been to include references to music and songs as they fit in with my dream journaling and general reflections upon my life experiences. These are usually experiences of synchronicity or precognition. For example, I was recently combing through my music library trying to identify a familiar piece of music that I had heard in one of my dreams. I was not sure what the piece was, only that it seemed to be from the Impressionist period of classical music from the early part of the twentieth century. A little later I went to the garage to do some other work, and when I turned on the radio, the very piece of music I had been trying to identify was playing. Music and the life of the spirit are interconnected, as are our dreams and the music we are hearing or performing in our waking lives, and we can document this in our journal. But that is a topic for another day—the importance of journaling is what I want to emphasize here.

Working with Your Dreams

Once you have settled on a method or methods to record and save your dreams, the next step is to begin to work more deeply with the dreams you recall. As a pastor, my first suggestion is that you take your dreams into your prayers. Ask God what a particular dream might mean for you or what the symbols in the dream might be saying to you. I'm often surprised by the way in which turning to God in prayer gives me insights about the subject of the prayer, whether immediately or later. Praying about a dream in the morning may lead to a flash of association or insight later in the day. Prayer is the first place to start working with your dreams if you are a person of faith.

You may also want to do additional dream work alone or with others. If you are working alone, much help is available. Read in the area of dreams and their symbols. The bibliography lists some of the books on this topic. The one caveat is that you must remember that only *you* know the meaning of your dream. You may get good advice and deep wisdom from books and other people, but the flash of "aha" when something strikes home for you is the best sign that you have found something helpful for your personal understanding of your dream. Some of the books in the bibliography promote this very kind of dream work. Others provide a wealth of insight, history, and wisdom about dreams resulting from people's curiosity about and work with their dreams. Some cultures have a particular place for dreams in their daily lives, and there may be insights gained from learning about these cultures and their use of dreams. But, and this cannot be said too often, the most reliable sign of insight into and understanding of your own dream is that "aha" of recognition when a particular association with an image or action in your dream speaks clearly to you.

This point is particularly important when it comes to the use of "dream dictionaries." These popular books are easily available in bookstores, supermarkets, and gift stores. They have a certain value, but the caveat mentioned above must always be kept in mind, that it is only your personal sense of rightness, that tingle of recognition or that sense of "aha," that will tell you whether the interpretation suggested fits your dream. The most helpful dictionaries will offer a variety of definitions or interpretations for each symbol. One person may agree with the classical interpretation of a particular symbol, but another may have a very different set of associations with the same symbol. My advice about dream dictionaries is to have several different dictionaries available so that you can compare the various interpretations.

Despite my reservations about dream dictionaries, I was in a dream group once where a member passed around a recently purchased dream dictionary. We looked at the definitions it had for a particular symbol that was being discussed that night. I had just given my standard qualifying remarks about the limitations of dream dictionaries. When I read aloud one of the definitions for the symbol in this particular dictionary, the dreamer had that "aha" of recognition with the association given in the book. That experience was an exception for me, however; I have often struggled with the rigid interpretations of images and symbols that dream dictionaries provide.

One of my favorite examples of the limitations of dictionaries or generally accepted associations with certain images or symbols is the symbol of an apple. Dreaming of an apple may mean something is coming to fruition, bearing fruit in your life. The biblical association with apples is a negative one, the apple being the forbidden fruit of the Garden of Eden. These are associations with apples that are part of Western culture. But there are limitations here. For someone with no knowledge or understanding of the Bible, this association will not fit. And, someone who is allergic to apples or has personal negative memories or associations with apples may have an entirely different association with the fruit. If you dream of an apple, which of the associations with apples fits for you? Only that tingle of "aha" will give you the answer.

Possibly none of the associations given for a particular dream image or metaphor will make any sense to you. One of the dangers of getting into dream work is that you can wind up spending so much time working with a particular dream image that it affects the rest of your life, taking time away from work, family, etc. When that happens, set the puzzling image aside and simply move on to other parts of the dream. A subsequent dream may shed light on the image that mystifies you. Something may occur in your life after the dream that will help you unpack that particular image.

A helpful tool for prayer and discernment that also works very well for dream work is the labyrinth, as described in chapter 7. If there is a labyrinth in your area, consider doing a labyrinth walk with a dream that you are working on. The process of walking a labyrinth allows your mind to "float" more freely, and when dreams are brought into the experience this free floating enables you to make associations to the dream contents more readily. Because dream contents can seem so irrational, associating more freely with images and symbols makes for better dream work. A labyrinth walk can be a good opportunity to make the connections between dream images and your deeper life.

When you feel you have reached the limit of your own resources, you may want to seek the help of other people. Of course, I encourage you to join a dream group. But, there are individuals with specialized training who may have particular insights about dreams that may be helpful to you, too. Many professional psychotherapists have specific training in understanding dreams. Likewise, spiritual directors may be familiar with the symbolic language that dreams use. Or, you may have a friend or relative you would trust with your dreams. Perhaps that person will be especially helpful since they know you well enough to have some insight about who you are. You will be able to tell who would be appropriate for you by their responses to you and your inquiries.

Safety is an important concern in dream work. How safe are you emotionally as you explore your dreams with someone else? Gauge your response to the possibility of working your dreams with another person based in part on how safe you feel. Are you comfortable with the responses of the particular dream worker you are considering, or is there something in their response that raises doubt for you? One helpful way to initiate such a conversation with a prospective dream worker is to suggest the method I favor for dream work, which is to begin any comment with the phrase "If it were my dream . . . ." This helps avoid the tendency many people have to tell others what their dreams mean. Based on the premise that only the dreamer knows for sure what their own dream means, this technique provides some protection from those who want to interpret your dream for you.

I recommend looking for someone to work with you on your dreams who is willing to subscribe to the ethics statement of the International Association for the Study of Dreams (IASD) (see appendix E). This statement spells out standards that I believe are important in doing dream work. The guidelines are designed to protect the dreamer, and they acknowledge the dynamics involved in working with dreams. The statement addresses the sovereignty of the dreamer, the risks inherent in tending dreams, the importance of the privacy of the dreamer, the qualification that dream work is not a substitute for therapy, and the fact that there are a number of equally valid dream work techniques and cultural specifics that may influence dream work.

My personal preference would be to do dream work with a member of the IASD, but I realize this may not always be possible. If someone belongs to the IASD, I believe you can then proceed with a certain level of trust already built into the relationship. If they are not a member, give them a copy of the ethics statement and then have a conversation with them about the statement and what your concerns are about doing dream work. Depending on the outcome of that conversation and your level of trust with the person, you may feel safe about proceeding. If the level of safety is not adequate for you, look elsewhere for a dream-tending partner, keeping in mind the level of emotional safety that is important for you.

The IASD provides many resources for working on dreams. The organization's main website, www.asdreams.org, has helpful links to online resources for dream work. The member pages link on the home page will take you to the people who are currently members and choose to have a member page. Some of the members have their own website, which lets you know their perspectives on working with dreams. One of the most helpful experiences for me is the annual conference put on by the IASD. These are five-day conferences offering a wealth of seminars and workshops covering the wide spectrum of work being done on dreams, including physiological research, psychological research, and spiritual research, as well as a great variety of techniques and methods for working with dreams. The website provides the schedules of recent conferences and, depending on the time of year, may list the schedule for the upcoming conference. One way to get additional help with your dream work is to identify a person who is presenting at the IASD conference on a subject that interests you and follow links to that person's website. Many dream workers have a section of their website that provides help for working with dreams, as well as helpful hints or links to other websites. The IASD is a valuable resource that is growing all the time and forming new regional groups in various parts of the world.

As discussed in chapter 3, I believe groups provide the best way to work with dreams. If one person can help you with your dream, four or five can help even more. So, how do you find a dream group? Depending on where you live, the nearest group may be in your town, in a nearby town, or several states away. Major metropolitan centers generally have dream activity going on. If it's appropriate for you, churches may be the best place to find a group of people interested in their dreams. Churches also frequently have ongoing small groups for support and education, which might include a group of people interested in exploring dreams together. You may need to look beyond your own local church or denomination. There are also centers of spirituality in a number of cities, some of which may offer dream-related activities. Such centers may focus on a variety of concerns, like feminist or women's centers, art and creativity centers, psychology clinics, adult education programs, local college programs, etc. Do an Internet search for dream groups in your general geographical area to find a local dream group.

If you are lucky, you will have choices in the style of dream group that you can participate in. If not, and you find yourself uncomfortable with what may be the only group in your area, consider staying in the group long enough to learn what you can. At some point, you might decide to start your own group. The appendixes give suggestions on how to do this, and you can find many helpful resources online related to pursuing the meaning of dreams and starting your own dream group. The best reference I know on starting a dream group is *Honoring the Dream: A Handbook for Dream Group Leaders* by Justina Lasley. If you are considering starting your own dream group, also think about attending one of the annual conferences of the IASD. Each conference includes several dream groups that meet every morning of the conference. Workshops offer many pointers and observations about various group techniques.

Having a professional person help as a mentor in this process is helpful, but dream groups do not need to be led by people with specialized training. A professional may provide much guidance about setting up a group and following the group guidelines, as well as be a resource when difficulties are encountered. Remember, though, that only the dreamer knows what his or her dream means; always adhere to this principle.

Group Projective Dream Work

The technique that I use in all my dream groups is known as Group Projective Dream Work. I learned this method from Jeremy Taylor.[1] Taylor explains the benefits of working with dreams in a group as follows:

> Because dreams always merge many levels of meaning into a single metaphor of dream experience, it is almost always productive to share dreams with people you care about and ask them about their dreams. When the multiple intelligences and intuitions of several people are brought to bear on a dream or series of dreams, it is much more likely that the dreamer will be exposed to a fuller range of the dream's possible meaning, and will have a chance to "tingle" and resonate to a wider spectrum of the dream's multiple levels and layers of significance. This kind of collective, group dream work is most beneficial to the life of the imagination and can nurture a community of creativity.[2]

Group Projective Dream Work provides a style of group work that has potential benefits for everyone involved. It embodies all the principles referred to in this book and carries the spirit of working with dreams that I recommend. The specific technique of dream work will vary from group to group and from group leader to group leader. The form of dream work I prefer and that seems easiest to use for beginning groups follows three steps. Before the group meets, it is best for the dreamer to write a narrative of his or her dream and have copies available for the group members. This keeps the narration clear in everyone's mind. The dreamer may change how they tell the story as they go along, but the written version gives group members something concrete to refer to.

The first step is for the dreamer to share the dream itself. If there is a written copy, the dreamer reads it to the group. The second step is for the group members to ask questions of the dreamer for clarification of the dream. The purpose of these questions is to better understand the dream's dynamics, emotions, and associations. For instance, if I name a particular relative or classmate or coworker, the questions of group members would be attempts to clarify the emotions involved for the dreamer. The group

---

1. Taylor credits Montague Ullman with developing this technique just before Taylor did. Ullman calls his method Experiential Dream Work. For more information, see Taylor, *Where People Fly*; Taylor, *Dream Work*; Ullman and Limmer, *The Variety of Dream Experience*.

2. Taylor, *Dream Work*, 76.

members are not trying to get inside the dreamer's life but to find parallel emotions and associations in their own lives so that they can make the dream their own. This can be a difficult process, particularly for those new to dream work. The function of this part of the group process is not for the other group members to interpret the dreamer's dream but to explore the dreamer's connections to the dream elements in order for the others in the group to make the dream their own at a deeper level.

The third step is the actual interpretation step, which is done a particular way in Group Projective Dream Work. Each group member's remark about the dream is prefaced with the phrase "If it were my dream . . ." or something very similar. The purpose of this is to emphasize the fact that the statement by the group member is their own projection, their own relating to the dream as if it had happened to them. This is a very important distinction. Ullman and Limmer explain this as follows:

> It is not easy to contain what I refer to as the "interpretive impulse," namely, the compulsion on the part of the listener to spontaneously and inappropriately offer an interpretive comment. We have to disavow any conviction we may have as to where the dreamer should go with the dream. It is difficult at times to restrain the tendency to validate through our questions our own impression of what the dream means. To do so is a breach of the basic rule that we follow rather than lead the dreamer. We have to rely on the dreamer's ability to make discoveries on her own to the extent she feels ready to after we have elucidated the context. We need to base the questioning only on what is obvious to the dreamer, that is, on what is in the dream or on what the dreamer has shared. Any question that is not obvious to the dreamer but that is derived from something in the interrogator's mind, is apt to raise the anxiety level of the dreamer (what does the questioner know about my dream that I don't?) and is self-defeating.[3]

Ensuring the emotional safety of all participants is an important part of the success of a dream group, and Group Projective Dream Work incorporates a layer of safety in the way the phrase "If it were my dream . . ." is used. Another benefit of this method is that the group members are able to have their own experience of the dream as though it were indeed their dream. Many times, with the help of the clarifying questions, I've been able to make someone else's dream my own in such a way as to gain some insights about myself. One of the variations of this method involves opening

3. Ullman and Limmer, *The Variety of Dream Experience*, 17.

the group by asking everyone in the group to share only the title and emotions of a dream, and then the group decides which of the dreams will be worked. By sharing the title and emotions of a dream, each group member participates personally, although briefly, in each gathering.

Group Projective Dream Work is a simple process that can be used to good effect by those new to dream work. If you are having trouble finding a dream group near you, this is a good technique to try on your own, provided you have a few people who are interested in doing dream work with you. Email can help isolated dreamers communicate with others interested in dream work. Searching the Internet for useful websites is one option for finding help with one's dreams. Other technologically assisted options are bulletin boards and chat rooms. If you are isolated geographically from either a dream group or a center that does dream work, it may be possible to work on dreams via one of these techniques in cyberspace.[4] I don't believe this to be the optimum method of dream work, but it can be better than nothing.[5]

The details of online dream work need to be worked out between the dreamer and the persons or group with whom he or she is working. A suggested method is as follows. The dreamer prepares a written narrative of the dream and also lists any clarifying material that came to the dreamer's attention, and then the dreamer sends this material by email or other online communications method to the partner or partners. The partners then respond with any clarifying questions that the dreamer did not cover. Then the interpretive phase begins, using the phrase and method "If it were my

4. The IASD has done considerable work in the use of computers and the Internet to facilitate dream work. An excellent survey of this work as of 2000 can be found at "Dreaming in Cyberspace," International Association for the Study of Dreams, http://www.asdreams.org/cyberdreams/features.htm. The articles listed on this page address various aspects of cyberspace as it relates to dream work.

5. John Herbert maintains that online dream work is *more* effective than face-to-face, or live, dream work. His rationale, summarized in an article by Richard C. Wilkerson, is as follows: "Why more meaningful responses online? The speculations centered on the asynchronous nature of this online group. That is, with a delay in posting the dream, the questions, the replies and the comments spread out over a week or two, the participants had time to ~reflect~ and give more considered answers. The dreamer had time to sift through the comments of others without any emotional group pressure to pick or judge the comments." Wilkerson, "John Herbert," para. 10. I find this reasoning very interesting and encouraging for geographically isolated dreamers. I would still maintain that face-to-face dream work is the best setting, however, particularly for members of a church, where more than just the dream work would be involved in the relationships between the group members.

dream . . ." Pictures and drawings might be shared electronically, as well. An online dialogue and conversation can be carried out just as would happen in a group where the members are physically present in the same location. The process will take longer than in person unless the group members are in a chat room or using something like instant messaging, where they are all online at the same time.

The one difference between "live" dream work and online dream work is the spirit that is present when people are face to face and present in the same room. The nature of digital communications and the effects it has on relationships is an area of increasing study and reflection. Guidelines and contract or covenantal details are being debated and discussed as this new means of communication unfolds.[6]

If you are uncomfortable with the dream groups in your area, are doing dream work by email, or are simply reading about dreams but are considering working with your own dreams, I encourage you to do your own dream work! For over twenty-five years, I simply recorded my dreams as regularly as I could and paid attention to the ways they "played" with my life and my prayers. If that is all you ever do, I promise that your life will be richer and you will sense the Spirit of God in your life in ways that will surprise you. It is worth the effort.

Acting on Your Dreams

I dream I'm in a boat with my son Luke in Lunada Bay, California. There is big surf outside but it is calm in the boat where we are. I see my friend Jack in an old boat out at one of the points of the bay, and he is going over the waves as they come in. Then he is caught inside a series of very big waves. I see several surfers riding these large waves, which now extend across the front of the bay. I never see Jack again and fear he has drowned.

When I awakened from this dream, I focused upon the character of Jack as I looked for what this dream was trying to tell me. My life was very busy at the time of this dream, and part of me feared being overwhelmed by the

---

6. My primary experience with digital communications as a pastor is with spiritual direction conducted by email. Workshops on online spiritual direction are held at nearly every conference of Spiritual Directors International (www.sdiworld.com). I have done some brief dream work via email that both I and the dreamers felt was effective, using the basic procedure outlined here. See appendix D for more discussion of online dream work.

press of academic studies and my full-time job as a pastor—the waves of my busy life were threatening to wash over me. That was a pretty simple interpretation and felt like it fit my life at that time. Later, a spiritual director helped me change my focus to being in the boat with my son Luke. She pointed out that if I changed my focus to what was there close to me, my son, I was in a calm place. This illustrates the value of having help working with your dreams, either from another person or a group. But beyond that, it pointed out a way for me to act on my dream. The dream reminded me to focus on my family, particularly my youngest son who was still at home, whenever I felt like my life was being overwhelmed by my work or my studies or the pressure to write a book or whatever else was going on. Simply remembering this dream would help me to calm down and feel less overwhelmed. This dream, and particularly its title, "In a Boat with Luke," became a reminder for me for several years about the direction I needed to look when overwhelmed with work. This was the way I acted on the dream.

In chapter 5, on the dreams in the Bible, I discussed the importance of Joseph and the Wise Men acting on their dreams. Acting on our dreams is just as valid for those of us who work with our dreams today. Doing something as a consequence of a particular dream helps the dreamer take the meaning and help of the dream into their life. My "In a Boat with Luke" dream suggests one of the easiest ways to act on a dream—simply remember the dream and the helpful message that you get out of it.

Note that I'm using the phrase "acting *on* a dream," not "acting *out* a dream." This distinction is important. We need to be careful not to literally act out dreams that may violate our moral or ethical code or break the laws of our society. Dreams of murder or other acts of violence, committing adultery, stealing, etc., are to be taken as symbols of something going on inside of us, not as instructions for ways to behave. I refer to this below in speaking of mistaken literalism in dreams.

Other ways to act on a dream are to make a drawing or collage of some part of the dream that speaks most deeply to you. Take your drawing or collage and post it somewhere where you will see it and be reminded of the dream on a regular basis. Perhaps some object in your life can serve in the same capacity. In chapter 7 I described a dream in which a series of images flashed by that had the color and warmth of icon paintings from the Orthodox Christian tradition. That was a powerful dream for me, and I acted on it by taking one of my favorite icons from my study and carrying it around for a few days. I then positioned the icon in a different and more visible place. I was reminded of the beauty and power of this dream whenever I looked at the icon. This is another way to act on a dream.

Sometimes, as in the story of Joseph and the Wise Men, a decision can be made on the basis of a dream. The dream that opens this book, titled "Deeper American Fork House" was the most powerful dream I've had in the last twelve years of my life. I dreamt of finding new rooms in the basement of the house I lived in in American Fork. Based on the dream and the subsequent work I did with it, I changed the direction of my ministerial career and my intentions for the remaining years of my working life. I acted *on* the dream—I didn't act *out* the dream. Had I acted out the dream, I might have chosen to visit the manse there in Utah, build a basement onto my current house, or even move back to Utah. But knowing that dreams use symbolic language, I explored what the symbols in this dream might mean for me. I took the symbolism of the basement of a church-owned house as symbolic of a call to deepen my own spiritual development. I did not move back to Utah or add on to my physical house; I went back to school and received training in particular spiritual practices. The presence of my in-laws was a symbol that my current wife would be involved in the process, as indeed she has been. This is a good example of the difference between acting on a dream and acting out a dream.

A caveat must be added here about acting out dreams. One effective way of working with a dream is indeed to act it out, to pantomime the actions in the dream, possibly with the help of others playing the role of dream characters. I've seen this done to great effect in workshops at IASD conferences, although this is not a technique I use with dream groups. Another way of physically acting out a dream, in a sense, may be the technique of drawing the dream in a dream group. I've seen good results for a dreamer when she drew her dream and the other members of the group drew it as well. This is a variation on the suggestion above of drawing or making a collage of the dream as a personal means of remembering it and carrying it forward with you.

As you become more comfortable with your dreams, you will find ways to integrate your dream life into your waking life. Based on dreams I've had, I have changed my sermons and I have come up with a new Vacation Bible School theme. I've titled phases of my life based on dreams. All these different ways to use dreams can be helpful as we seek to integrate our dream life with our waking life. They are all ways of acting on our dreams.

Mistaken Literalism

One of the issues faced by those who begin to work with their dreams is what I've learned to call 'mistaken literalism.' This term came from a Spiritual Directors International conference I attended where Jeremy Taylor spoke about dreams in spiritual direction.[7] Taylor used this term to describe how we tend to err when we take dream actions and images literally and not as the symbols and metaphors that they are. For example, if we dream of dying, murdering someone, committing adultery, or any of a number of other behaviors that would shock us or offend our moral sense in waking life, we must look beneath the literal action to the symbolic action to find what the particular dream might be saying to us.

My favorite illustration of this issue of mistaken literalism can be found in the New Testament. In Matt 5:29–30, Jesus says

> "If your right eye causes you to sin, tear it out and throw it away; it is better for you to lose one of your members than for your whole body to be thrown into hell. And if your right hand causes you to sin, cut it off and throw it away; it is better for you to lose one of your members than for your whole body to go into hell." (NRSV)

If we took these words of Jesus literally, we would all be in trouble, walking around blind and missing a hand. But we know that Jesus is speaking metaphorically. That does not make Jesus' teaching here any less true or effective. Indeed, I believe it makes it more so. In the same way, we must not take the more disturbing images and actions in dreams literally. We need to look beneath the surface and try to find what our dream might be saying to us. Savary, Berne, and Williams also talk about this idea of mistaken literalism, though they don't use that term for it: "Symbolic dream language expressions such as murder, execution, rape, incest, abortion, and so on are to be treated as *symbolic expressions of inner energy*, not as a literal statement which would be viewed as immoral or illegal in outer life."[8]

The issue of immoral actions portrayed in a dream will be discussed briefly in the next chapter. Another way to think of the issue of mistaken

7. Taylor, Plenary Address, SDI26-002.

8. Savary et al., *Dreams and Spiritual Growth*, 146. The authors continue: "People with very weak egos or under great psychological stress may interpret such dream content literally and may try (or feel obliged) to act it out. Certain people are afraid of their dreams because they fear that the strong symbolic dream action may actually happen in their outer lives. This is why working with dream symbols as inner experience can relieve persons of unnecessary insecurity and anxiety." Ibid., 147.

literalism is to consider a particularly bizarre activity that is portrayed in a dream, such as flying, being in two places at once, or dreaming of being in your childhood home but the place looks nothing like your childhood home looked in reality. These are the kinds of dream experiences that give dreams their sense of strangeness and can prompt curiosity about dreams and their meanings. In the case of the unfamiliar childhood home, for example, we may be tempted to dismiss the dream as just a weird confusion of dream and reality, a kind of silliness, but that would be to suffer from mistaken literalism. What I suggest to people in such situations is to note the differences in the dream between what you recall about your childhood home, for example, and what is portrayed in the dream. Begin to look at the details of the dream image. How is it different from your actual childhood home? What are the specific differences? Do any of them have any associations for you, any connection to current events or other events in your life? Many dream workers whom I know use this "space" between what the dream portrays and what the reality is or was as the place to begin to do the work on the dream. Is there some message in the difference between the dream and reality? Is there something from your childhood memories or experiences that might be of use to you in your waking life today, something that this dream may be trying to tell you?

We live in a world where literalism is the prevalent method of understanding. But when we make the shift into the world of dreams, we need to move away from literalism to find the deeper messages that our dreams may be trying to give us. Once this threshold of mistaken literalism is crossed, our ability to work with dreams and profit by them grows greatly. The same can be said for our understanding of the Bible, as is discussed in chapter 8 on the relationship between the Bible and the language of dreams. In the latter case, once we can begin to discern what is to be taken literally and what is metaphor or symbol, our understanding of the Bible will increase and its ability to speak to our lives will deepen.

Difficulty Recalling Dreams

Dream recall is one of the stumbling blocks many people experience when they first try to work with their dreams. Everyone dreams, but many believe they don't dream because they do not recall their dreams. For lots of people, that's fine because they have no interest in recalling their dreams. For those who have been captured by their dreams, or have had some particularly powerful dreams and want to pursue their dreams, dream recall becomes important. After all the years of recording my dreams, recall is not difficult for me, but I see it as an issue for others in dream groups, particularly those who are just beginning to work with their dreams. The suggestions and techniques covered in this section are those I have found to be effective for dream group members.

Chapter 1 included a brief discussion of the physiology of dreaming, noting that we cycle through periods of sleep that produce various levels of dreaming. If dream recall is an issue, learning about the cycle of sleep is a good place to start. The period of sleep known as REM (Rapid Eye Movement) is the period that seems to produce the most dreams. So, one option to improve dream recall is to time your waking to coincide with the REM cycle. REM takes place about every ninety minutes, on average. The longest period of REM sleep occurs between 6½ and 8 hours of sleep. For the average night's sleep, this occurs just before the time to wake in the morning; this will often be the period when you have dreams that you remember. If recall is a problem for you, you might want to structure your waking pattern to facilitate this last REM period. Whether you sleep at night or during the day, the ninety-minute REM cycle will provide a guideline for you.

You can also work on the other end of the sleep period, the beginning of your sleep time. If you can wake up about ninety minutes after falling asleep, you will have a good chance of recalling dreams. One way to do this is with an alarm clock, setting it for about ninety minutes after the onset of sleep. A more natural way that I've practiced is to take a large drink of water before going to bed. That will necessitate waking to go to the bathroom after about ninety minutes, and you will likely find yourself waking out of a dream. You can make your notes at that time, and chances are good that you will fall back to sleep easily. The ninety-minute REM cycle is a good gauge to use to determine the most likely times when you will be dreaming. I've even heard of people setting their alarm clocks for every ninety minutes throughout the night to facilitate their dream recall. That seems excessive to me, though, particularly for those of us who have jobs to get to in the morning and desire a good night's sleep.

In addition to the REM periods, there are two specific periods when we can prompt better dream recall: the time when we go to bed and the time when we awake. When we go to bed, there are a variety of techniques we can use that might improve our recall. For those of us with a faith practice, we can pray we will have better dream recall (we can pray for specific elements in our dreams too, like guidance, comfort, or inspiration, but here I am only considering dream recall). We can pray simply that we will recall our dreams, that God may have something to say to us through our dreams and that we want to hear it. Varieties of auto-suggestion may work too, like telling ourselves we want to recall a dream we have tonight or that tomorrow we *will* recall a dream we have tonight.

Praying for a dream is a version of the ancient practice of dream incubation, which refers to following a ritual to generate a dream. Incubation has been practiced to generate a dream to answer a particular question or give guidance to a situation in waking life. The ancient Greeks used dream incubation for the purposes of healing. The Bible makes reference to King Solomon incubating a dream in 1 Kgs 3:3–15.[9] I think of incubation as a way of "programming" the mind to recall dreams. I've done this by simply writing out a question or subject or even just a word on a piece of paper and placing it under my pillow.[10]

The other period when we can work to improve dream recall is the period immediately upon awakening. If we get a healthy, normal stretch of seven or eight hours of sleep, the longest REM period of the night will come just before waking. It is important to try to capture something from that period if we are not accustomed to recalling and/or recording our dreams or if we are having trouble with recall during a certain period in our life. In dealing with dream recall issues, learn not to move too quickly after waking. Our minds are accustomed to shifting from sleep and the dream state into the tasks at hand. This shift is an important place to pay attention. Many people recall that they have been dreaming, but in the few moments it takes to get up and begin to think about the day ahead, the dream recall slips away ever so quickly. One way to counter this process is to lie in bed for a few moments after waking. Focus backwards. What was the last scene of the dream, the one from which you awoke? What happened before that? And before that? Changing your position in the bed to the various

---

9. See chapter 5 for a brief discussion of Solomon's dream.

10. The most dramatic experience of this came to me when I was focusing on the female characters in my dreams and using the Jungian concept of the anima to see them as representations of my soul. One day a dream worker I was working with asked me what the name of my anima was, and I had no idea. That night I put a note under my pillow that read, "What is your name?" Among my dreams that night was this one: *I'm in a room, trying to get through a tight space between a corner that juts out and a couple of chairs that are right up next to the corner. A woman named Susanna is sitting in the one that blocks my way, so I ask her to move her chair.* This was a very indirect reference to a woman named Susanna, but I took it as a very clear answer to my incubated question.

positions that you sleep in sometimes stimulates a memory. An image of someone you know may pass through your mind as you wake up, and that may be a clue to what you were dreaming. Your sleeping partner may be able to help you with dream recall, particularly if they either go to sleep or wake up earlier than you do. Ask them to look at you every few minutes. If they see you twitching in your sleep or notice that you're having rapid eye movement while you sleep, they can gently wake you and ask what you were dreaming.

Some other ways to improve dream recall include the following:

- Accept and value each dream, regardless of how foolish or fragmentary it may appear at the time. It may fit into a larger pattern that will only become apparent later.

- Select an unpressured period of several days, such as a weekend or vacation, to focus on improving your dream recall. Allow yourself to awaken spontaneously from a dream rather than by alarm clock or some other disruption to your natural cycle.

- Share a dream with a friend. This sometimes helps set the memory of the dream and leads to insights as you describe it. Joining or creating a dream group almost guarantees dream recall. Be sure to write down your dreams, however, so you have a record for comparing past and future dreams.[11]

Another suggestion is to recall the dreams that you have already had. Reading or reviewing your dream journal as you prepare to go to sleep may be a way to slip back into the river of dream material that makes up your own life.[12] Consider reading poetry or looking at symbolic art that specifically uses symbols and images more than literal representations of the natural world. The key is to stimulate your mind toward the symbols and images that it uses for dreams in the hope that you will be ready to recall dreams when you wake up.

These are some techniques that can be used if dream recall is difficult for you. Once you get in the habit of recalling and recording your dreams, recall will become easier. You may go through periods of no recall

---

11. For additional suggestions, see Garfield, *The Healing Power of Dreams*, 20–23.

12. This suggestion comes from Craig Webb, a Canadian IASD member who works with dreams. His website, The Dreams Foundation, is http://www.dreams.ca. One of the links on his webpage discusses dream recall techniques; this is located at http://www.dreams.ca/recall.htm.

alternating with periods of rich recall that produce several remembered dream scenes from each night. Periods of less recall may reflect the stress of a particular time in your life, your exhaustion, or some other temporary factor. You might just ignore short periods of no recall. If the lack of dream recall persists and you are concerned about it, you can begin with the suggestions given here.

The Borderlands of Dreams

Three scenes: a visual scale that adjusts the rate of dying of characters in a video game; a bicycle floor pump that dances around the floor; a work prioritizing list.

Dream work: These are all day residue from yesterday and last night— my son's video games, watching TV, and a church meeting I was thinking about.

The above dream narrative and the related comment serve as a portal into what I call the borderlands of dreams. This term refers to the periods between sleep and waking, which are called the hypnogogic and hypnopompic stages of sleep. Hypnogogic refers to the period between waking and sleeping as one is falling asleep, and hypnopompic refers to the period between sleeping and waking as one awakens in the morning. The above dream narrative is composed of hypnopompic scenes.

You may be familiar with hypnogogic activity. As you are falling asleep, you suddenly jerk your legs, or gasp, or your body convulses briefly. My understanding of this state is that the brain has not yet completely shut off its motor functions as sleep begins, and thus brief dream scenes still elicit some motor activity.[13] These are interesting to me but I have never devoted energy to exploring them. I'm focused on getting to sleep and fear that the interrupting of sleep onset to note these hypnogogic dreams would keep me awake. This is an area of sleep that is of interest to lucid dreamers (see discussion of lucid dreams in chapter 1). I've heard lucid dreamers

13. Hobson puts it this way: "One of the most instructive examples of state boundary crossing is the tendency to experience dreamlike visuomotor sensations at sleep onset. These are called hypnogogic hallucinations if the subject is still awake enough to notice or be aroused by them." Hobson, *The Dream Drugstore*, 153. Hobson also writes about hypnopompic dreams, as well as false awakenings, out-of-body experiences, alien abductions (!), narcolepsy, and other sleep disturbances.

speak of holding themselves in the hypnogogic state for a long period, thus enabling them to practice more of the techniques of lucid dreaming.

The area of borderland dreaming that I do work with is the hypnopompic realm of dreaming. Most of these brief scenes are simply day residue. I experience more hypnopompic activity whenever I lie in bed, either returning to sleep or just lingering in getting out of bed. I make the notes anyway, just to keep a log of what I dream about. Occasionally, a hypnopompic dream scene will speak to powerful issues going on in my life, but that is the exception.

The reason I mention this material on the hypnogogic and hypnopompic stages of sleep is that as you begin to notice your dreams, you may encounter these stages of sleep and notice the level of dream activity that takes place at each of these stages. Also, if you are having difficulty with dream recall, focusing on the hypnopompic activity may be an aid to deeper dream recall. In that case, you would recall, and perhaps make note of, any hypnopompic dreams and then try to recall what preceded them, until you become better at recalling dreams from the various periods of the night.

In the next chapter, I address the precautions or considerations that need to be taken into account as you begin to work with your dreams.

10

Challenges in Dream Work

I dream I'm walking down the sidewalk where I grew up in the direction of my parents' home. On the right side of me is the park and on the left is my elementary school. The park is bright with an overwhelming light, but something inside of me tells me it is not safe or good. There are several people at the park smiling at me and welcoming me, but I do not feel safe because they are strangers. There is darkness to the left of me, but I feel safe in it because I can recognize the people; some are family and friends. Also, the whole time that I am in this dream, I hear the voices of people talking to me, but I do not understand what they are saying.

Dream work is not for everyone. The dreamer who shared the above dream dropped out of the dream group after just a couple of meetings. I wondered why that was. There are elements of fear and threat in this dream, to be sure, related to the people in the park. Even though these people are smiling at her, their being strangers seemed to frighten or threaten her enough to outweigh what the rest of the dream group saw as positive associations and images in the dream. But, the dream also includes strong elements of safety and security, of welcoming and hospitality, in the darkness, contrary to what one might expect. The dreamer recognized people on the dark side, and she was drawn to the darkness. For this particular dreamer, the elements of fear and threat far outweighed any beneficial or helpful elements. I tried to point out to her that the more positive and helpful images could be a counterforce to the negative images. The whole group worked in this direction, but to no avail. We left off working on the dream fairly early in the process that night.

This dreamer returned to the next group meeting with a similar dream, one that included negative images that the dreamer saw as threatening. Yet, some images of help and support again provided a way to work positively with the dream. For reasons the other members of the group never understood, this dreamer could not see the balance between positive and negative images and the way the positive images might not only outweigh the negative but could also have provided a way to grow personally from the dream. To the group's credit, they worked hard to encourage this dreamer, as did I, but she did not return to the group after these two experiences. There seemed to have been nothing the group could do to work with this person's sense of fear.

How does one work with such a dream? In any situation where there is a sense of threat or danger, particularly if it comes from either side or from behind the dreamer in the dream, one of the first responses in dream work is to turn and face the threat. If it is a creature or a person, the dreamer may ask the threatening image, "What do you want from me?" This can be a very fruitful experience, and new growth can come to the individual from doing such dream work. This is easier said than done, however. In the above dream narrative, I was struck by the fact that the strangers were smiling at the dreamer. If it were my dream, I would see those smiles as inviting me to explore what these strangers had to offer me. But, this approach to dream work is not for everyone.

In order to participate fully in dream work, dreamers must be convinced there is value in working with dreams, that paying attention to our nighttime experiences offers an opportunity for better self-understanding, personal growth, and spiritual growth. In addition, we must be truly open to finding out about ourselves and our feelings. We must believe that personal growth and growth in faith can come from facing the unpleasant things in our dreams. Indeed, growth can come from facing unpleasant things in all realms of life. Dreams offer us a deep—but not direct—way to face ourselves. The interested dreamer must be willing to believe that the benefit gained from dream work will outweigh any unpleasantness they may encounter in the process of the work.

Deep but Not Direct

Dreams reveal the deepest parts of ourselves, but they do it in ways that, at least initially, are not very confrontational or threatening. They are deep but not direct. As we work with our dreams, we will discover various levels of meaning for us in any one dream. We can take the meanings we are comfortable with and leave the other meanings for later, if we choose. We do not recall dreams that we are not ready or willing to deal with. As we face our dreams, we may become increasingly able to uncover all they have to tell us and will get much help from them. But, we may not be ready for all that our dreams can tell us. The freedom we have to choose whether or not to work with all the elements of a dream is a freedom we can move around in. By this, I mean that we can work with the part of the dream that we understand right now and then return to the dream later to work it further, to work the deeper parts of it, the parts that we are not comfortable with or that we didn't understand at all when we were in the initial phase of working with the dream.

As I noted in the first chapter, some people have recurring dreams. These are dreams that start out gentle and mild. If we are willing to work with our dreams, such dreams may lead to resolution of an issue in our life that the dream is trying to address. If we ignore the dream, we will find that we have recurring dreams that give us a similar message. If we ignore these recurring dreams, the images in the dreams may become more and more frightening until the dream takes on the feelings of a nightmare. The deep parts of ourselves revealed in such dreams gives us repeated opportunities to address whatever the issues are that are being revealed.

In a supportive dream group, we can explore parts of ourselves that we might be uncomfortable exploring on our own or in less supportive circumstances. Deep and serious personal issues can be uncovered in a dream group, ones that are beyond the ability of the group or the leader to work with. When that happens, it is appropriate to refer the dreamer to therapy to work on those issues. In my years of doing dream work, however, both individually and in group settings, I have not encountered a situation where referral to a professional psychologist was needed, although that kind of referral might have been of great value to the dreamer who is referred to in the opening of this chapter. But in the great majority of cases, a good supportive dream group is able to handle whatever comes up in group members' dreams. The deep but not direct ways that dreams work give us the ability to work with them, provided we have a comfortable and safe environment.

Life Stage

The ages and life experiences of dream group participants should be considered when working with dream groups. Jung observed that the ways we are able to examine or reflect upon our lives has to do with our stage of life. In the first stage, which comprises roughly half of our life, we are busy establishing our place in the world—growing up, marrying, starting a family, and starting a career. The second stage of life has to do with integrating our values and experiences, 'making sense' of our lives and either discovering or further cultivating the meaning of our lives. This second stage is the stage of soul work. It is during this second stage of life, in the Jungian schema, when we are most interested in matters of the spirit and when dream work can be of the most value.[1]

This does not mean that dream work will not be of interest to us in the first stage of our life, but it does mean that our reasons for doing dream work may vary depending on the stage of life we are in when we engage in it. Here's an example. As a part of her senior project for high school, a teenage girl had been involved with a church dream group that I led. All the other members of the group were older women aged fifty and up. At one point I was explaining the Jungian concept of anima and animus to the group. I mentioned that when there are female characters in the dream of a male and that female character has some kind of 'charge' to it, we can be relatively safe in concluding that this is an anima figure, a symbol representing the soul. Likewise, for a female dreamer, if there is a male figure in a dream and there is an extra charge to that figure, we can assume that this is an animus symbol, a soul image for that dreamer.

The high school student then asked if that would be the case for her, too. I explained that it might be the case but that she was in a different stage of life and it would be of benefit for her to consider the particular dream image from a wider variety of possibilities than just the animus type. Because she was still finding her way in relationships, particularly relationships with the opposite sex, she would be working through different issues than those of us who had been married or involved in a long-term partnership. I did

---

1. Robert A. Johnson puts it this way: "Generally, the first half of life is devoted to the cultural process—gaining one's skills, raising a family, disciplining one's self in a hundred different ways; the second half of life is devoted to restoring the wholeness (making holy) of life. One might complain that his is a senseless round trip except that the wholeness at the end is conscious while it was unconscious and childlike at the beginning." Johnson, *Owning Your Own Shadow*, 10.

not mean by this that the older folks in the room had figured out all the dynamics of relationships. Indeed, all of us humans continue to work on the issues raised in our relationships throughout our lives. But in terms of the dream work we were involved in, it was helpful for this teenager to consider some different or additional associations for male dream images in her dreams.

Need for Self-Reflection

I've noticed that the initial excitement of some people about working with their dreams fades as they realize they will have to do some self-reflection, some inner work when they pay attention to their dreams. I use the term "curiosity factor" to describe their initial enthusiasm. People sometimes start out with an interest in the meaning of their dreams but turn away from the deeper work that dreams invite them into. The curiosity factor is what leads some people to think that learning about dreams might be interesting and fun. They might think they will gain a certain amount of wisdom or power by learning about their dreams. Perhaps they think they will gain great topics of conversation at parties. There is much popular interest in dreams, as evidenced by articles in the popular media, particularly magazines, which usually emphasize the more spectacular aspects of dreams or the dramatic role that dreams have played in historical events.

This curiosity factor works well up to a point. When the dreamer's interest reaches the level of deeper personal reflection, a decision has to be made. Does the dreamer want to pursue his or her dreams to the point where it begins to require some inner work, some introspection, some self-honesty? For some people, the answer is no. For them, dreams become too much 'work'; they take too much energy. There may be issues in their lives that they do not want to face or deal with, even at the cost of remaining a less healthy or less balanced person. It may be a matter of fear or of simply not wanting to expend energy in that direction. In any case, it is always the dreamer's choice to decide what they will do with their dream.

If we do choose to pursue dream work, it is helpful for us to remember that our psyches, our souls, will not remember a dream that we cannot deal with. There seems to be a kind of indwelling safety or protective mechanism built into our dream life. If a dream is remembered, we have the resources to deal with its content and meaning. I believe that our dreams are there to help us grow, to heal us.[2] This can be a great comfort when we are struggling with particular material in our dreams. But, it is a comfort that we have to grow into.

> *My childhood friend Steve is in the car with us, and he takes a little boy who is misbehaving and hangs him out the window, holding him by his legs. We all shout at Steve to pull the boy back in. He does, but the boy is profoundly traumatized; it seems he was mentally or emotionally unbalanced to begin with, and the look in his eyes tells me that this trauma has caused him to revert back into a kind of catatonic state. The woman who is driving pulls over, a Swedish guy takes over driving, and the woman holds the little boy and tries to comfort him. Then, I wake up.*

When we run up against something unpleasant in our dreams, as in the above dream narrative, our basic instinct is to turn away from it. But, it may be this very thing, this bit of unpleasantness, that ends up producing the most insight for us. This dream narrative was the last part of a longer dream I had. I woke disturbed by the way the boy was treated, and I remained disturbed for some time after waking until I worked with the dream. There were options for me as I worked the dream. Does the story of the little boy represent a scene I had witnessed a couple days before of a parent behaving in a way I considered inappropriate toward a child in a grocery store? Does he represent some part of me that I am mistreating? Does he represent my nine-year-old son, whom I may be mistreating by neglecting him due to my busy work schedule? In my waking life, I would never dangle a child out a car window by his legs. So, the dream action on the surface is repulsive to me. But, working with the dream gave me helpful insights into my life and my relationships, insights that I could use to modify my behavior in a more positive direction.

If we are only curious about dreams, we might readily turn away from an unpleasant dream like this, dismissing it as behavior we would never engage in. It takes dedication and a commitment to personal growth through understanding our dreams to stick with the images that make us uncomfortable. This necessity for dedication and commitment is what I am highlighting here. It is easy for someone who is experienced with dreams and dream images and language to be able to face disturbing dreams and

---

2. Taylor, *Where People Fly*, 10. I take my inspiration for the healing properties of dreams in part from Taylor. One of his major points, nearly the first thing he says about dreams, is that "all dreams come in the service of health and wholeness." Ibid., 5.

know that working with them will yield something of value. They trust their dreams to be able to help them, no matter how repulsive the images. But for those who are starting out and do not yet trust their dreams, the fear or anxiety generated by frightening dream images may be enough to turn them away from further pursuing the meaning of the dream (the discussion of mistaken literalism covered in chapter 9 is relevant here).

Our Moral Code and Dreams

I dream I was in some sort of program and we were learning how to handle weapons. Someone was sitting high up on a ledge and was aiming his gun at me, and I raised my gun and shot and hit him right in the forehead. He looked really surprised and then fell over. I was very upset that I had killed him. *I was telling my husband I thought we all had blanks. Enrique [one of my students] came over very excited and told me that if I had not gotten that person, think of how many others he might have shot.*

I wrote about this dream in chapter 8. The section that is not italicized here is the part of the dream relevant to this discussion. This dreamer was upset, even in the dream, about her violent action. In her commentary on it, she said, "Even when I woke up in the morning I was still feeling sick to my stomach, and typing this made me feel sick." Her action in this dream violated her moral code so deeply that she was physically affected. It is against her personal moral code (not to mention a violation of the Ten Commandments!) to commit murder. What's going on in this dream?

We must be ready to suspend our moral code in dream work. We do not have to change our moral code, but we do need to remember that dreams communicate in symbols and should not be taken literally. We should be careful of mistaken literalism, as discussed in the previous chapter. Such a conflict with our moral code can be another hurdle to overcome for those new to dream work or those beginning to consider the meaning of their dreams. One of the first rules to remember about dreams is that they use the language of image and symbol. The above dream happens to be about murder, but dreams of adultery, suicide, theft, bribery, etc., would also violate the moral code of most dreamers. We would not commit these acts under normal circumstances, but such acts do occasionally appear in our dreams. In the first years I worked with my dreams, I was upset and even revolted by some of the things I appeared to do in my dreams. But I persisted in recalling my dreams and doing dream work because, despite the unpleasant or immoral aspects of my dreams, I found much that was helpful and supportive of my spiritual life. This setting aside of one's moral code is not something everyone can do easily or is interested in doing.

As discussed in chapter 3, a dream group may be very valuable in a situation like this. Other members of the group are always able to see more of the dream than the dreamer. In the case of the above dream, group members were able to help the dreamer see beyond her emotional reaction of horror and disgust in order to look at what the dream said to her about her relation to the person she killed in the dream. The dreamer found great relief in the help the other group members were able to offer, and I believe she was then better able to handle future dreams where morally repugnant activity took place. The challenge is to look past the literal, morally troublesome aspects of the dream and get to the symbolic message behind them. In this example, a good approach would be to ask what in the dream indicated that the dreamer was 'right on target' with something in her relationship with the person she shot. There can indeed be pay dirt in some of the more disturbing parts of a dream.

Psi Phenomena

I'm driving three people from my congregation around Southern California, in the area of Long Beach and Palos Verdes. We go up a long hill that seems like a nice Northern California hill—open space with houses dotting the area but not packed closely together. We get up on top of the hill and I comment on the lovely view we have, with the harbor down below us, a mountain across from the harbor, other mountains behind to the left, and a city off to the left. I think it's supposed to be Los Angeles, but it looks nothing like that city in reality. There is a large round tower building between us and the harbor that looks like the Capitol Records building in Hollywood—circular and about twenty stories tall. It could also be the large circular condo building in downtown Long Beach.

This narrative is part of a longer dream that had considerable power for me and woke me up before my alarm went off, but this particular scene had the most energy for me in subsequent weeks. I had recently put together a selection of concerts for members of my church to attend together, which took about two months of planning, ticket purchasing, etc. The program meant a great deal to me because it brought together my love of music and my desire to use that love in some creative way in my ministry. I was heavily invested emotionally in the program. On the day of the final concert of the program, we drove across Los Angeles from Whittier to the campus of the University of California, Los Angeles. This concert took place about a month after I had the above dream. As we rounded a bend in the freeway, there was a large round tower building off to the side of the freeway. I immediately recalled the dream of the month before, the dream in which I was driving parishioners and saw a similar building in the distance. This was one of the more memorable and powerful pre-cognitive dreams I'd had in a while.

Pre-cognitive dreams are one of a group of phenomena called *psi,* as in psychic phenomena. These are discussed in chapter 8 in the section on dreams and the language of prayer. Psi experiences, by their nature, defy the rules of rationality, and for those new to dream work they can be problematic to face and work with. For those of us who live mostly in the world of rationality, encountering psi experiences can be unnerving. My psi experience in the dream shared above might have frightened me were I not already fairly familiar with psi experiences after decades of dream work and study. As I comment in chapter 8, the more we work with dreams, the more often we have these kinds of experiences. There is no current scientific explanation for these psi experiences, which can lead to difficulties, or perhaps embarrassment, for those who have experienced them and talk about them.

On the other hand, the sensationalism and the allure of psi experiences can add other blockages to our getting involved with dream work. We can get caught up in the fascination with psi experiences, treat them simply as a conversation topic, and stay away from what the psi experiences might be telling us. It is very important to remember that once we start doing dream work with any regularity, psi experiences will happen to us with increasing frequency; we need to accept that fact and understand it in whatever way is comfortable for us.

Related to this, I have a personal theory of the experience known as déjà vu, which is when we feel that we have been in a particular situation or place before or have already had a particular experience but cannot remember when or where. There is an eerie feeling associated with déjà vu, a sense of mystery, because it feels very real but we cannot rationally explain it, nor is it under our control. My personal experience over the years has been that déjà vu is a function of dream recall. In other words, we have dreamt of the place, situation, or feeling that prompts us to feel déjà vu. After years of keeping track of my dreams, now when I have an experience of déjà vu I can recall the specific dream that is related to the particular experience. This means that the dream is a pre-cognitive dream. There is a tingle of excitement when I recognize this, somewhat like the tingle of eeriness that happens with déjà vu, but it is a different kind of excitement for me because I can recall the dream in which I dreamt of the place or experience that I later am living in my waking world. Some of the dreams and experiences already described in this chapter were pre-cognitive dreams that were related to an activity that I was involved in. I have not yet seen this explanation of déjà vu offered in the literature I have read on dreams or psi experiences, but I believe it is a plausible explanation.

The important question for me in relation to pre-cognitive dreams is, what is it about this experience that I need to pay closer attention to? This is where our paying attention to our dreams pays off, encouraging us to use our dreams to better understand ourselves and the way we are living our life, the way we are being faithful to God, or however we define our own sense of integrity.

> *Then I find myself in what seems like a middle school or high school, with several single-story buildings with hallways, etc. Suddenly I'm alone, and I remain alone for the rest of the dream. Someone is coming down a hallway near me, and I realize it is someone who is pursuing me. I stand behind a door around the corner from the hallway where the pursuer is. When the guy comes in, I see he is mentally disabled or mentally ill. He walks right past me. I realize I'm in a mental hospital or training center for developmentally disabled people.*

This was the third part of an extensive dream I had that consisted of six parts. It was a very powerful dream that woke me up early and filled me with such energy that I was not able to get back to sleep. I walked about in a daze after waking, as though still in the state of the dream as it ended; it felt as if I was either one of the developmentally disabled people or was pretending to be as an alternative way to live. I was so struck by the dream that I carried it around with me for a few days, trying to come to some understanding of it.

The above dream narrative was the part of the dream that spoke most powerfully to me in the weeks and months to come. I had the dream about ten days before attending an annual conference of the International

Association for the Study of Dreams (IASD) in Massachusetts. While participating in a morning dream group at the conference, I found myself in a corner of the room, and when I looked around the room, there was the door and the wall from my dream of ten days before. I felt the great rush of the excitement that always accompanies my recognition of a waking manifestation of one of my dreams. Had I not recalled that specific part of the dream, I'm certain I would have interpreted the experience as déjà vu. As it was, I worked with that dream each morning in the group, looking at the corner and wall from different angles, walking around the room and replicating my roles and actions in the dream as well as those of the person who had seemed to be pursuing me in the dream.

What was it I needed to pay attention to in this dream, including its pre-cognitive aspects? In the end, what I got out of this part of the dream was a confirmation of what I was doing with my life, particularly my working with my dreams. In that way the dream was a soul-confirming dream. The experience of recognizing part of a powerful dream while at an IASD conference was a signal to me that I was where I needed to be, that my participation in IASD was being confirmed by that deep part of me that produces dreams. I believe that God was confirming this action and this direction in my life. What might have been to others an experience of déjà vu was to me an experience of recalling my pre-cognitive dream in which I had a quick glimpse into my future, which confirmed and reinforced the direction I had taken with my life.

Dream Work Narcissism

Little Jack Horner

sat in the corner,

eating a Christmas pie;

He put in his thumb,

and pulled out a plum,

and said "What a good boy am I!"[3]

The next pitfall of dream work that I want to address is what I refer to as "dream work narcissism." I have always understood the nursery rhyme "Little Jack Horner" as a warning against thinking too much of oneself.

---

3. Opie and Opie, *The Oxford Dictionary of Nursery Rhymes,* 234.

The ancient myth of Narcissus conveys the deeper implications of this human tendency; Narcissus fell in love with his own reflection and ended up dying. By dream work narcissism, I mean an unhealthy obsession with our own dreams and what they might mean, getting so involved with our dreams and ourselves that we begin to have little time or interest or energy for other people; we may get so caught up in ourselves, our dream life, our 'personalized' images, etc., that we become increasingly self-centered and self-focused. In such a situation, there may be no room for God's Holy Spirit to break through. My understanding of dreams is that our dreams themselves will tell us when that kind of unhealthy behavior begins to take its toll. Indeed, the signs will appear in our dreams even before such behavior becomes a negative force in our lives.

> *I dream I'm traveling in Minnesota with my wife and son. My son is off at a movie somewhere, and my wife is off on her own on a tour. I'm trying to buy a ticket for the light rail, whose cars look like the old red streetcars from Los Angeles, so I can meet them at the airport. I look down a flat area between some very steep hills and see open flat plains stretching out to the west. It's dark, and when I look up I can see thousands of stars, as though I were in the mountains or somewhere else with no streetlights. It's absolutely wondrous. There are a couple of people standing behind me, and I wonder to myself if they realize what a blessing it is to live near such beauty. I'm thinking that Minneapolis is nearby and that, since it's a much smaller city than Los Angeles, there is less light to cut off the view of the stars. Then I go around the corner of the station house and come upon a car full of older women being joined by two more. Everyone in the car is singing the hymn "Softly and Tenderly." Several of the singers look right at me. I go inside to buy a light rail ticket and have to go up to the counter and ask the people behind the counter for help. There are no signs explaining the prices, times, destinations, etc., of the trains. There is lots of food for sale, though; the counter looks more like a bakery than a ticket counter. Finally, someone directs me to the left to buy a ticket. As I start to move that way, I notice a huge black woman behind me, well over seven feet tall, who has two children with her. She doesn't move aside for me, and I have to push my way past her, telling her I need to go down to that end of the counter. I wake up.*

I could have spent the whole morning exploring the symbols and associations in this dream. Why Minnesota? What was the meaning of my traveling with my wife and son? What associations do I have with stars? Who are the women in the car? Why that particular hymn? What tickets did I want or need? Why the huge black woman? Each one of these images in the dream could have led to significant reflection and research, and I was eager to do so, but the needs of work and family called me away. I had two more dreams that week about tickets, so I decided that tickets were the major symbol to be considered, but I never did go back to work on the other details in the dream.

Not all dreams are as rich in symbols and contain so many potential resources for research and study. But, if one recalls two or three dreams each night, the cumulative amount of dream material can become quite large. One simply cannot work with it all. Perhaps if one is independently wealthy or retired, one can find the time to do extensive dream work. But, for the average person, the demands of daily life limit the amount of time available for dream work. Job, family, school, volunteer work—any number of activities pull us away from working on our dreams.

For Christians, in particular, the danger of getting too focused on our dreams can interfere with our spiritual life. Most of us are called into the world—into relationships, into work and school, and into families—in order to serve each other in the world and to serve Christ through each other. Our dreams are a wonderful way to understand ourselves and the world around us, giving us another source of information. But, from the Christian point of view, if we are not using that increased understanding and information to serve others, we are not being fully faithful to our religious values. Ours is a faith of actions, not simply beliefs, and of deeds, not just dogma.

Matthew 7:21–29 reminds us of the importance of acting on our faith, not just talking about it. Dream work can be an exciting adventure, and we can get lost in the excitement of it, particularly as we begin to experience the psi phenomena. Our understanding of dream symbols, our experience with psi effects, and our comfort with the realm of dreaming can all be sources of pride and offer us opportunities to boast. Such behavior is inappropriate in a life of faith in Christ. But the connection between biblical faith and dreams is one that cannot be ignored. The fact that God can indeed use our dreams to help us on our faith journey is something we can appreciate and be grateful to God for. Being surrounded by brothers and sisters in the faith and in the church is a good way to hold ourselves accountable to each other, to keep our faith on an even keel, to maintain a balance between inner life and outer activity. Dreams are one of the best ways to maintain our inner life, but we need the balance, the corrective, of our call to serve the world.

Related to dream work narcissism is what happens when dreamers get carried away with themselves and have too great a sense of self-importance. One of the characteristics of cult movements is the sense of self-importance of the leaders and, conversely, the lack of self-esteem of the followers.

The idea that dreams are special revelations of God or of a higher power that then enable the dreamer to tell others what to believe and how to run their lives is one manifestation of the dangerous side of dream work. History, particularly the history of religions, is full of examples of people who have interpreted their dreams as special revelations of the divine to them and them alone. They see their dream activity as a special dispensation enabling them—indeed, ordaining them—to be unique agents of the divine. All manner of abuse, injustice, and violence has been inflicted on others due to such delusions.

Dream Work and Low Self-Esteem

The reverse of the kind of megalomania that characterizes narcissism is the low self-esteem that might lead the dreamer to totally discount their dreams as having any meaning for them. This is different from the belief that dreams are nonsense, merely a misfiring of the chemical activity of the brain while we sleep. What I speak of here is the belief that dreams may be important but that only the dreams of other people, not of oneself, are significant. Dreamers with low self-esteem may have nights full of wonderful, enriching, and insightful dreams, but if they don't believe that they themselves might be the recipients of such help, the value of their dreams will go unrealized.

I argue for a rational approach to dreams and a balanced incorporation of dreams into the devotional life of the "ordinary" Christian. The power with which dreams may speak to us is very real and can be life-changing, as illustrated by numerous examples in this book. But the danger of megalomania comes when we think that our dreams mean that God is choosing us to be a special messenger of God to the extent that we have the right to tell others how to live and that we are therefore exempt from the levels of accountability and responsibility that apply to all people everywhere. There are other psychological dynamics going on here, and dreams are used to further those dynamics in such cases. I'm reminded of some of the biblical injunctions against dreams, such as Deut 13:1–5 or Jer 23:25–32.[4]

4. Both these texts are discussed in chapter 5.

The flip side of this is the idea that dreams are only valuable for famous historical figures or great religious leaders, which is a belief held by people with low self-esteem. This manifests itself in relation to dreams and dream work as the attitude that "my dreams don't mean much, certainly nothing like the dreams in the Bible or the dreams of great Christians." In contrast, participants in dream groups often realize that their dreams are indeed like those of characters in the Bible or important people in church history. Our dreams speak to us in the same way dreams have spoken to people throughout history. They can give us the sense of the immanence of the world of spirit, just as they have done throughout human existence. We may not become famous people or great religious leaders, but we can have the same sense of God's presence in our lives as well-known people of faith. Let us not think too little of ourselves, and let us pay attention to our dreams in such a way as to discover what God is saying to us through them.

In relation to thinking too much or too little of ourselves, dream groups can be a great aid. The members of a dream group can help us keep a sense of balance between our dreams and the world around us. A dream group can help keep in check the tendency to think that our dreams make us better, more enlightened, or closer to God than others. On the other hand, group members can help us see that there is indeed a message for us in our dreams.

An additional layer of support can come from the church. As covered in chapter 2, holding a dream group or dream work in a church helps set the context of faith for the work. As I noted earlier, the church can act as a *container* for dreams and dream work. The tradition of the Christian church, and its use of the Scripture as a guide, can provide a check for those who think too much or too little of themselves. In the same way, Scripture and tradition remind us of God's desire to be with us, to guide us and accompany us in our life. Our dreams can be a convenient and reliable help in discovering that guidance and accompaniment.

Resistance in the Church

Having said that the church provides a container for dreamers and dream work, I should also mention that there is often resistance in the church to taking dreams seriously and doing dream work. Because dreams and dream work are not mainstream practices in contemporary Christianity, those who choose to use and work with their dreams in their spiritual practice may face particular challenges. As I have pointed out, there is a long tradition of doing dream work in the church, despite this contemporary resistance. Both attitudes are present in the church today, and dreamers seeking to work with their dreams as a spiritual practice should expect to encounter that resistance.

My approach to dreams is that of a minister ordained in a mainline Christian denomination. I take seriously the insights brought to our human lives by the work of great psychologists like Freud and Jung. Some Christian denominations or local churches, however, discount anything that is not in the Bible or in their tradition that specifically recommends working with dreams. People have said to me things like, "All we need is to know the Word of God [the Bible and its teachings] and then we will have all we need for salvation." Included in this viewpoint is the teaching of the Bible that the day of prophecy has passed. The sense here is that dreams were once vehicles for God to speak to the prophets, but that time is long gone. Dreams are viewed as too subjective and emotional and as potentially leading us away from the truth of what God has to say to us. As I mentioned in chapter 8, however, I believe that one of the values of dreams is their ability to help us understand the Bible better. I do not argue with people who are expressing resistance to dreams when I encounter them in more conservative churches. People are rarely convinced of the truth of something merely by argument.

An argument that I've encountered in more progressive or liberal churches is that dreams are just the misfiring of the brain while we sleep and therefore should not be given any credence. This is a more "modern" or "scientific" version of resistance to dreams. This perspective on dreams is more likely to be held by liberal religious people than by conservatives. I place myself in the spectrum of church expressions in our culture in the liberal contemporary mainline church, so I can speak from my direct experience. It seems to me that we are sometimes more captivated by sociology and mass psychology than by theology and spirituality. I believe dreams offer ready access to the world of the spirit. If a person is not interested in the world of the spirit, for whatever reason, then dreams will not hold much appeal for him or her.

My experience is that the resistance of liberals is essentially the same as that of conservatives, although for different reasons, and thus the resistance will feel the same to dreamers looking for support in understanding their dreams. The precaution here is simply for the dreamer to be prepared for some resistance among brother and sister Christians and Christian leaders. One of my hopes for this book is that it will open up the world of dreams and dreaming to those who might have felt some resistance to doing dream work in the past. I would like to make a special appeal to clergy. Even if you are not interested in your own dreams, being open to dreams and dream work can only help your ministry. This book can be the first step in your helping your church members to faithfully explore the world of their dreams.

Keeping in mind the limitations outlined in this chapter, you can decide if dream work and using dreams in your spiritual life is something you want to pursue. There may well be other particular challenges unique to you as the dreamer, but the ones I address in this chapter are the ones I've encountered in my dream life and in working with the dreams of others. The kind of dream work I promote has to do with the daily promptings that dreams provide in our spiritual lives. There is a richness to be explored in our dreams that can be found in few other places, but, like any other spiritual practice, it requires us to be able to reflect honestly about our life. We must enter this world with our eyes open and play with the images. The rewards to be had from working with our dreams can be immense.

11

Dreaming into the Future

In the last days it will be, God declares
that I will pour out my Spirit upon all flesh,
and your sons and your daughters shall prophesy,
and your young men shall see visions,
and your old men shall dream dreams.

—Acts 2:17, quoting Joel 2:28

Nearly all the wisdom we possess, that is to say, true and sound wisdom, consists of two parts: the knowledge of God and of ourselves.

—Calvin, *Institutes,* 1.1.1

I t is tempting to believe that the dream work many people are engaged in today is a powerful fulfillment of the prophecy from Joel that people will be prophesying, seeing visions, and dreaming dreams. It may turn out to be so, if future generations look back upon this time and see that our paying attention to dreams opened new ways for God's spirit to move among the faithful and the world. However, every time of great change and upheaval in Judeo-Christian societies is accompanied by the same desire to see clear evidence of God's guidance in the midst of the changes and turbulence. Dreams are a manifestation of God's spirit in our world today. But, I suggest that we hold lightly the ultimate significance of our dreams and our dream work. Dreams and our working and playing with them can be very helpful, but to say that this moment in history is the most important revelation of God's power and spirit since New Testament times reflects spiritual self-centeredness.

I'm much more comfortable acknowledging the ways our dreams add to our knowledge of ourselves and God, as John Calvin emphasizes in the above quote. These words open Calvin's monumental work that had a great influence on the history of Western Christianity, particularly the religion of those who settled America. The knowledge of God is what the discipline of theology is all about. The knowledge of ourselves is what medicine, psychology, sociology, and a host of other disciplines are engaged in. Calvin was open to the knowledge that these other disciplines might provide in our lives of faith. [1]

The premise of this book is that dreams provide us with a way of learning about ourselves and therefore can contribute helpful wisdom to us as we move through life. Powerful dreams that can be seen as God-given revelations in the lives of dreamers do occur. But, I believe that most dreams are meant to help us in our daily lives and our daily struggles with faith. Dreams have long been a neglected source of help, a neglected source of knowledge about ourselves and God, even though they are readily accessible to us, have been with us since before history began, and are universally available. Being comfortable and familiar with our dreams and working with them, even if only occasionally, provides an additional source of information about ourselves and the world around us.

I believe the information our dreams have for us can best be revealed in a group setting. We all tend to be blind to ourselves; thus, we can get a better picture of ourselves, more knowledge about ourselves, with the help of a caring group. That knowledge is not secret knowledge, although it takes some effort to learn the language of dreams. It is not necessarily God speaking to us, although that can happen in our dreams. Our dreams are there for a purpose, the reasons for which are lost in the mystery of the creation of human beings. As Robert White noted in 1975, "Although modern research has increased our knowledge of what goes on in the sleeping state, it seems in no way to have robbed dreams of their mystery or stripped them of their allure. Their study and interpretation continues to be a field with a future."[2]

The future interest in dreams that White spoke of over forty years ago is evident today. There are some areas related to dream work that I believe

1. See the discussion of Calvin's attitude toward dreams in chapter 6.

2. Artemidorus, *The Interpretation of Dreams*, vii.

bear further exploration but are outside the purview of this book. I will mention these areas briefly in this concluding chapter.

Physiological Sciences

The development of increasingly sophisticated and accurate measuring devices has enabled scientists to analyze and study the dreaming process as it takes place in our brains. The level of precision that is now achievable would no doubt astound the original discoverers of REM sleep in 1953.[3] The debate between the scientific community, which tends to see dreaming as merely a physiological reaction, and the religious or spiritual community, which attaches importance to the meaning of dreams, appears to be a debate that will continue into the foreseeable future. I hope the proponents of each view will learn to cooperate, perhaps by supplementing each other's findings. This cooperation may be happening in certain small ways, but I am not aware of much publicity about such collaboration. Even at International Association for the Study of Dreams conferences, where members of both the scientific and the spiritual communities are present, there does not appear to be a lot of conversation between the two groups.

Kelly Bulkeley, in his book *The Wondering Brain*, "seeks a deeper understanding of wonder by means of a new integration of religious studies and cognitive neuroscience."[4] This is the kind of integration that I believe we will see more of in the future as scientific exploration encounters religious experience and vice versa. As that encounter takes place, I believe that dreaming and its physiological components can play a role in exploring the way humans are created and how we view and interact with the world around us. How this encounter unfolds will be of interest to dreamers, and the way we use our dreams may change. But, at this point, I believe we can continue to use our dreams to our own spiritual benefit, as outlined in this book.

3. Even though REM sleep was "discovered" in 1953, there is evidence that the ancient Greeks were aware of the rapid eye movement that takes place during dreaming. Other mentions of this phenomenon are scattered throughout the history of dream commentary.

4. Bulkeley, *The Wondering Brain*, 3.

Psychological Sciences

The psychological sciences have also paid increasing attention to the religious realm of human experience in recent decades. Moving away from Freud's understanding of religion as neurotic behavior, an increasing number of psychologists are now deeply interested in the realm of spirituality. In my own profession of ordained ministry, I've noticed the way the most recent generation or two of clergy have incorporated psychological insights into ministry. In fact, many clergy have moved into second careers as trained psychological counselors, often setting up psychologically based counseling centers and services in local churches.

Psychology and religion both can draw on our dreams as a resource. Bulkeley provides good insights into the interface between psychology and religion or psychology and religious experience.[5] Many contemporary psychologists and psychoanalysts, however, lack an interest in dreams. Followers of the psychological school centered on the work of C. G. Jung tend to be the only counselors who use dreams in their techniques. This is an area that bears further investigation.

Dreams are dealt with differently when used for therapy than when used for growth. Just as there was a popular movement among clergy some twenty-five years ago to incorporate pastoral counseling into their

---

5. According to Bulkeley, "Over the last century, Western psychological science, from the depth psychologies of James, Freud and Jung to the brain-mind marvels of contemporary CN [cognitive neuroscience], has established a solid foundation of knowledge regarding what Kant calls the 'invisible self' and what we have been speaking of as the 'unconscious.' We know, first and foremost, that ordinary consciousness is aware of only a miniscule portion of all that is happening in the brain-mind system at any given moment. A tip of an iceberg, a tiny island in a vast ocean, a candle in a great dark room—these timeworn metaphors remain accurate portrayals of the fundamental fact of human psychology. We know, furthermore, that shifting a person's state of consciousness can bring into awareness new previously unknown portions of the unconscious (this is how our knowledge of the 'invisible self' develops, by systematically correlating many different reports from many different states of consciousness). We know more now than ever before about the nonconscious workings of perception, emotion, memory, reasoning, language, and imagination. We know that the drives and desires of the unconscious can come into conflict with each other, and we know that they can also join together in surprising harmonies of creative power. We know that consciousness has some degree of freedom to guide its own drives and desires, and we know that this flexible "executive" capacity for selective attention and volitional action can be powerfully shaped by interpersonal relationships, cultural symbols, and social institutions. Humans are innately inclined to aggression, deceit, and selfishness, but we are also predisposed to cooperation, friendliness, and caregiving." Ibid., 192.

ministry, today there is a similar interest in spiritual direction. I have seen this shift among therapists as well, who often speak of the need of many of their clients for spiritual help in addition to the healing brought through therapy. As a consequence, the number of therapists receiving training in spiritual direction has grown. As a trained spiritual director myself, I have watched the discipline of spiritual direction take firm root and grow among Americans of various religious persuasions and of no particular religious persuasion at all.

The distinction between therapy and spiritual direction that I find most helpful is to consider therapy as aimed at healing and spiritual direction as aimed at growth. Dreams can be of benefit in both areas. Dreams can help us heal from past hurts, if the therapist will work with our dreams. But if spiritual growth rather than healing is the main focus, then dreams and dream groups can be a very helpful tool. The realm of dreams and dream work is an area of common ground that the fields of psychological counseling and spiritual direction can and should share.

Psi Experiences

Another area that would benefit from further exploration is that of psi experiences, which I discussed in chapters 8 and 10.[6] The sensational aspects of psi catch people's interest. For example, a growing number of television shows depict psi experiences that contribute to the plot or feature characters who possess a specific extra-sensory ability that they use to help solve mysteries or resolve relationship issues. This exploitation of psi is popular, and these programs keep the sensational aspects of psi in people's awareness. On the other hand, reputable institutes and groups are studying and documenting psi, and this may lead to psi experiences gaining more legitimacy in today's scientific and rational world. The increasing sophistication of scientific instruments enables the measurement of our body and brain functions in ways that are unprecedented.

Our experiences of psi phenomena increase as we pay more attention to our dreams. Many dream workers I know will attest to this. But, to be able to scientifically validate or verify these experiences and their connection to dreaming is beyond our ability with contemporary scientific methods.

6. Chapter 8 addresses psi in the discussion of the language of prayer and chapter 10 in the section on the allure of psi as a potential pitfall to be aware of before beginning dream work.

Those of us who have these experiences and connect them to our dream lives will be able to compare new research findings with our own experiences. I see an interesting parallel here to the realm of religious belief. As a Christian, my faith in God cannot be scientifically proven, but it is one of the determining factors in my life. Likewise, my experiences of psi cannot be scientifically proven. Will there be a breakthrough in scientific research that will verify the currently unprovable experiences of dreamers and other people? I hope to see breakthroughs in both these areas during my lifetime.

One of the significant characteristics of psi experiences is their universality. Many people can recall a time when they thought of someone they had not heard from in a long time and within a few days received a letter, phone call, or email from that person. No one can validate the mechanism by which this happens, but enough people have had these experiences to strengthen the popular understanding of the truthfulness of these kinds of psi experiences. In relation to more unusual psi phenomena, Jeremy Taylor suggests that examining experiences such as alien abductions, past-life experiences, reincarnation, and channeling in relation to the realm of dreams and dreaming could be beneficial.[7] Because of the prevalence of psi experiences associated with dreaming, these other fields may become of more interest to people in dream groups in the future.

Personal Prayer Images

I discussed the practice of praying with icons in chapter 7. I would like to see further research and practice in this area by people familiar with both icons and dreams. I believe our dreams offer a system of personalized images through which God is able to communicate with us. That is my faith-oriented belief. I first recognized that dream images can be personal icons when I began a practice of praying with icons, those beautiful pieces of art that play such a large role in the spirituality of members of the Orthodox Christian tradition. I have since taught a course in church on the practice of using icons for prayer. Henri J. M. Nouwen says, "Every time I trust myself to these images, move beyond my curious questions about their origin, history and artistic value, and let them speak to me in their own language, they

7. See Taylor, *The Living Labyrinth*, 53-58. I'm not saying that Taylor believes that these experiences can be fully explained by considering them as dimensions of dreams and dreaming, which was my first impression when I read his book. This whole field is much more complex than that.

draw me into closer communion with the God of love." I would say exactly the same thing about the images in our dreams. [8]

There are other uses of images in prayer and meditation, such as a particular approach to prayer developed by St. Ignatius.[9] There is also a relatively new practice called "visio divina."[10] In this practice, which strikes me as a cross between spiritual direction and therapy, the focus person is asked to move into a meditative, calm state and then look for God coming to him or her in an image. This image may be a parent, an ocean, a lion, or other images unique to the person praying. As Karen Kuchan describes this practice, it is a conscious, deliberate seeking of or working with an image.

My experience is that our dreams provide us with tailor-made "God-given" images that speak to us powerfully and deeply because they are directly personal. Ignatius's technique leads us more immediately into the Bible and the stories there, which Christians are at least somewhat familiar with if not profoundly shaped by. This is a conscious, deliberate process. Praying by gazing upon icons can lead one into associations with the characteristics of God that are meant to be represented by the icon. Again, this is a conscious, deliberate process. In both dreams and the Ignatian exercises, the conscious and deliberate approach is meant to move one toward a more free association with the images or settings. The same can be said about visio divina in that one is consciously and deliberately pursuing a revelation from God. I'm reminded, however, of Parker Palmer's description of our soul being like a wild animal. He says, "If we want to see a wild animal, we know that the last thing we should do is go crashing through the woods yelling for it to come out."[11]

Dreams come to us unsought. Though they may be incubated or induced, they will happen whether or not we ask for them. They bring us messages that we often do not hear otherwise because the messages do not necessarily fit into our conscious plans, the agenda of our waking world. As such, I believe dreams offer us more immediate and personalized value than other prayer practices. Those who have some experience working with their own dreams report repeated images in their dreams that feel

8. Nouwen, *Behold the Beauty of the Lord*, 15.

9. Ignatius instructs us to imagine a particular scene from the Bible and put ourselves into that scene, hearing the noises that would be there, seeing the other people that might be there, smelling the odors, etc. Ignatius of Loyola, *The Spiritual Exercises and Selected Works*, 146–59.

10 Kuchan, "Visio Divina," 22–23.

11. Palmer, *A Hidden Wholeness*, 58.

tailor-made for them. I have also seen this in dream groups that have been meeting together over an extended period of time. When people have been working with their dreams and begin to see specific patterns or repeated images in their dreams, these can be seen as personal dream images. There is evidence that dreams functioned in this way among Quakers during the colonial period. Dreams served that particular community because they were convenient, easily shared, and indeed portable in ways that other means of assisted prayer were not.[12]

With the exception of the material just quoted, I have found little written about personal prayer images. According to Joyce Rockwood Hudson, "The fact is that no other person, however highly trained, can ever understand a dream as well as it can potentially be understood by the one who dreamt it. Your dreams use your own language to talk about your own life in terms best suited to your own particular consciousness."[13] Hudson alludes to self-knowledge here. I would add that self-knowledge makes for the most honest prayer. Since our dreams can aid us in being honest with ourselves, they can help make our prayers more honest and hence more effective. This is the connection between our working with our dreams and the statement by John Calvin that wisdom is knowledge of God and of oneself. This is another reason for us to reclaim the power and gift of our dreams.

Dreams and Mysticism

Why not be a mystic?[14] This is an intriguing question for members of the church today. Karl Rahner wrote, "The devout Christian of the future will either be a 'mystic', one who has 'experienced' something, or he will cease to be anything at all."[15] I maintain that our dreams, especially when we work with them in a group setting, give us the kind of experience that Rahner

12. Carla Gerona writes, "Unlike most iconic paintings, dreams were imminently moveable. But like paintings, dreams could provide powerful narrative, spiritual, and emotional frames that guided believers on spiritual and mundane journeys. Even in jail one could conjure up a dream to endure a difficult situation and perhaps even to try to change it. Dreamwork thus could work as an alternative to other more visual spiritual aids, whether a painting or a cross. Dreams indeed resembled pictures and artifacts because like them they helped elicit, channel, and direct spiritual feelings." Gerona, *Night Journeys*, 72.

13. Hudson, *Natural Spirituality*, 86.

14. This phrase comes from a book of the same name by Frank X. Tuoti.

15. Rahner, *Theological Investigations*, 7:15.

refers to. Rahner was not speaking of dreams specifically but of a Christian faith that is more than intellectual, more than just a 'head trip.' Our dreams help us get out of our head and live our faith on more than just an intellectual level. Our dreams help us know ourselves better, help us set priorities in our lives, help us with our prayer life, and help us become more familiar and comfortable with the Bible. All these are qualities that help us be better Christians, and all would, I believe, fit into Rahner's definition of the experience of being a modern mystic.

Mysticism has not always enjoyed a good reputation, particularly among Protestants. But as more and more Protestants have moved into the realm of spirituality, the writings of the mystics of centuries past are becoming more relevant to today's people of faith. The relationship between dreaming and mysticism has not yet been thoroughly studied.[16] My personal experience, however, and that of others I have worked with both inside and outside of the Christian church, is that dreams provide the deeper level of living, personal reflection, and meaning in life that religions aim at. Why not try it? Why not be a mystic?

The process of recalling and praying about our dreams deepens our spiritual life. Our dreams are not God speaking to us, though God can speak through our dreams. Our dreams are not the secret to our life, though they can reveal much about ourselves that we may not otherwise discover. Our dreams are part of who we are, and, as such, they will benefit our spiritual life inasmuch we offer them to God, just as we offer to God the rest of our life. I offer this book to God and to the church as we seek to be faithful where we find ourselves. May God bless the seed that is planted here in the lives of dreamers in the church.

16. See Bulkeley, "Mystical Dreaming," 30–41.

Appendix A

Starting Your Own Dream Group

If you have been paying attention to your own dreams, writing them down, working with them the best you can, doing some reading about dreams and how to understand them, and maybe even talking with others about your and their dreams, you can start your own group. Yes, you can!

The first thing you should do is obtain a copy of *Honoring the Dream* by Justina Lasley. This book is a "must have" for anyone contemplating starting a dream group. It is relatively expensive, but I consider it indispensable for dream group leaders. It includes very practical guidelines and suggestions for deciding if a dream group is something you want to do, group guidelines, group problem solving, group techniques, and a wealth of other material helpful in beginning and leading a dream group.

In this book I primarily discuss dream groups in churches, but you can start one in your home or at a community center, local bookstore, etc. In considering a particular location, think about the messages that might be conveyed by your hosting a dream group in that venue. What might that location symbolize to others? If you hold a dream group in a counseling center, for example, will people think you are doing dream work for healing? People will approach you and their dreams with different expectations when they are seeking healing versus growth (see my discussion of this in chapter 8).

Here are some suggestions for starting a dream group in a church.

- Propose starting a dream group in your church directly to the pastor or pastors of the church.

- Propose the dream group as a spiritual practice, similar to learning to pray, doing lectio divina, walking a labyrinth, praying with the psalms, etc.

- Propose a regional dream group to your presbytery, district, diocese, or whatever the larger organizational level of your denomination is. Perhaps your local town has a clergy association whose membership crosses denominational lines. If so, propose a regional dream group to members of this association.

- To build interest in a new dream group, talk about dreams in group and one-on-one interactions with congregants and write about them in church newsletters and website articles and other forums.

- Promote a dream group as an evangelistic opportunity as well as an opportunity for growth. People who might not be interested in church from a religious point of view might nevertheless be interested in joining a dream group that is held at a church. Church members and non-church members in the dream group will form relationships, and this may lead the non-member to participate in other church activities.

- Establish a code of confidentiality for the group. If participants discuss a particular dream outside the group, they are to ask the permission of the dreamer first and to do so in such a way that the dreamer cannot be identified. In general, group members should not talk about what goes on in the group with people outside the group.

Appendix B

Guidelines for Writing a Dream Report

This is a standard format for dream reports prepared by members of a dream group who have a dream they want to share with the group.

1. Type the narrative of your dream up or handwrite it as legibly as you can. Please include your name (first name only, if you prefer) and the date of the dream.

2. As you record your dream in writing, use the present tense, as in "I am running down the street" not "I was running down the street" or "She is flying through the trees" not "She was flying through the trees."

3. Give your dream a title, if you wish. The title may change as a consequence of the work done on the dream, but choosing a title can be a helpful initial step in the process.

4. Try to describe the dream without reflecting upon it. Describe any feelings that you had during the dream or upon waking up from the dream.

5. After you have written the dream narrative, please add whatever background information the rest of the group will need to get a better picture of the dream's place in your life. Include things such as who the various characters are in relation to you, what associations you make with objects or places in the dream, and any other information that will help the others in the group "get inside" your dream. You may also bring a related drawing, watercolor, collage, or any other visual aid with you to the dream group meeting.

6. Bring enough copies of your dream report for each member of the group.

Appendix C

Suggested Process for Dream Groups

This is a suggested process for each meeting of your dream group. You may find other suggested approaches in your reading. Develop a format that feels most comfortable to you. Justina Lasley's book *Honoring the Dream* is the best source for ideas on this topic. Once your group gets going, you will find the style that is comfortable for you, and you can be flexible and adapt to the situations that are brought to each particular group gathering.

Check-in

This is part of the social functioning of the group. Ask, "How is everyone doing? Are there any comments or questions about previous dream work or other dream issues?"

Opening prayer or ritual

You might use a candle, icon, cross, or piece of dream-inspired art as a centerpiece.

Tending to the group members' dreams

Ask if anyone would like art materials so they can draw their dream.

> *Circle of title/feeling.* In this transitional exercise, each group member shares a title and the associated feelings of a dream they had, but no work is done on it. Alternatively, each member may tell a

dream during this time. Through this exercise, the group enters into the realm of dream; it is a warm-up that helps participants prepare to work their dreams on a deeper level. It also enables each participant to feel they are part of the group even if their dream is not worked deeply at that gathering.

Select the dream(s) to work on during the gathering. The group chooses the dream or dreams they want to work based on the initial sharing of title, feelings, and dream narrative. If there are several dreams to share, you might want to divide the allotted time by the number of dreams and impose a time limit for each dream. Normally, ten minutes is the minimum to give to a dream, but more time is better. I know several groups where only one dream is worked per group session.[1]

Work the dream(s) chosen for the session. Here is the general process I use in working with a dream in a group:

- The dreamer reads the dream out loud, once or perhaps twice. Handing out copies of a written dream narrative (see appendix B) can be very helpful.

- The dreamer shares his or her associations and connections to the various images and parts of the dream. This is the work of the dreamer.

- The group members ask clarifying questions to help them make the dream their own. This involves asking the dreamer about images or parts of the dream that he or she may not have given background to in their presentation of the dream. These are questions for clarification, not statements of interpretation. The goal here is for the group members to be able to understand the emotions and history of the dreamer in order to be able to relate to a part or parts of the dream. This is the work of the group members.

- Once the dreamer and the group feel ready to move on to the next stage, the group members respond with statements like "If it were my dream . . ." or "In my version of the dream . . ." or something similar. This is the part where the group members offer interpretations of the dream. More questions for clarification may come up during this part of the process.

---

1. This is the case with the Ullman method of dream work, described in Ullman and Limmer, *The Variety of Dream Experience*, 3–29.

This continues for the time allotted or until the dreamer feels that enough has been done with the dream to satisfy them for the present. Some dream sharers may feel overwhelmed with the amount of interpretation and may need to simply listen to all the feedback and work with the dream on their own later.

- A key point is that it is always "dreamer's choice" in the process. That is, it is up to the dreamer to decide if he or she wants to investigate a dream further in a particular direction with the group. There may be some emotions or memories the dreamer would rather not share with the group. The group should always respect the desires of the dreamer.

- When it feels like the work on the dream has reached a concluding point, the dream group leader asks the dreamer if there is anything more he or she needs. Then the leader may ask the dreamer how he or she intends to incorporate or act on the work of the group on their dream.

Questions or comments for the whole group. At the end of the session, ask if there are any questions or comments from the group as a whole. This may be about the work that was done in the session or group scheduling issues or whatever else the group might want to discuss. Agree on the next date for the group to meet.

Closing prayer or ritual

This is the end of the evening and brings the dream group session to an end. Depending on how the group opened, there may be a closing prayer or some words said as the candle is extinguished. Each group usually comes up with its own opening and closing rituals.

Appendix D

Online Dream Work

Jeremy Taylor, mentioned throughout this book, offers occasional training programs for online dream group leadership, and I participated in the first one of these that was offered. I found the process of doing dream work through video conferencing interesting and very workable. Taylor's program that I participated in was made up of experienced dream group leaders and dream workers. The experience the group members had with leading dream groups gave us a head start on the online process because we were all comfortable with dream group processes and etiquette. The major challenge for us was the use of the video conferencing platform—the technological details. Doing online dream work with people new to dream groups and dream work would present challenges beyond the technological issues, however. The procedures and etiquette of dream groups take some practice, and I'm not sure how comfortable people new to dream work or dream groups would be with learning this online. Another drawback I see to online dream work is that body language and emotional subtlety cannot be read or felt as easily as when group members are physically present with each other.

People are becoming more and more experienced with video conferencing and online learning and training. Many families already carry on regular communications with video conferencing programs, and family members of all ages participate. Grandparents today are learning to use computers and then moving on to video conferencing, just to stay in touch with their children and grandchildren. So, it is likely that people will be increasingly willing to try online dream groups. Also, online dream work is an excellent way for people who live in isolated areas to get involved with dream work in a way that they would not otherwise be able to do.

Appendix D

Everything in this book is relevant to both in-person and online dream groups. I encourage you to take your dreams seriously and to use the tools I have given you to work with your dreams. Whether you do that work in the physical or the virtual presence of others, the suggestions and guidance I offer in this book are relevant to your dream work with others.

Appendix E

International Association for the Study of Dreams (IASD)

Dreamwork Ethics Statement

IASD celebrates the many benefits of dream work, yet recognizes that there are potential risks. IASD supports an approach to dreamwork and dream sharing that respects the dreamer's dignity and integrity, and which recognizes the dreamer as the decision-maker regarding the significance of the dream. Systems of dreamwork that assign authority or knowledge of the dream's meanings to someone other than the dreamer can be misleading, incorrect, and harmful. Ethical dreamwork helps the dreamer work with his/her own dream images, feelings, and associations, and guides the dreamer to more fully experience, appreciate, and understand the dream. Every dream may have multiple meanings, and different techniques may be reasonably employed to touch these multiple layers of significance.

A dreamer's decision to share or discontinue sharing a dream should always be respected and honored. The dreamer should be forewarned that unexpected issues or emotions may arise in the course of the dreamwork. Information and mutual agreement about the degree of privacy and confidentiality are essential ingredients in creating a safe atmosphere for dream sharing.

Dreamwork outside a clinical setting is not a substitute for psychotherapy, or other professional treatment, and should not be used as such.

IASD recognizes and respects that there are many valid and time-honored dreamwork traditions. We invite and welcome the participation of dreamers from all cultures. There are social, cultural, and transpersonal aspects to dream experience. In this statement we do not mean to imply that the only valid approach to dreamwork focuses on the dreamer's personal life. Our purpose is to honor and respect the person of the dreamer as well as the dream itself, regardless of how the relationship between the two may be understood.

Prepared by the IASD Ethics Committee
Carol Warner, Chair
Association for the Study of Dreams
Spring 1997

Source: http://www.asdreams.org/idxaboutus.htm#ethics1. A shorter ethics statement is also available on this webpage.

Bibliography

Altman, Jack. *1001 Dreams*. San Francisco: Chronicle, 2002.

Artemidorus. *The Interpretation of Dreams (The* Oneirocritica *of Artemidorus)*. Translated by Robert J. White. Torrance, CA: Original, 1975.

Artress, Lauren. *Walking a Sacred Path: Rediscovering the Labyrinth as a Spiritual Practice*. New York: Riverhead, 2006.

Bar, Shaul. *A Letter That Has Not Been Read: Dreams in the Hebrew Bible*. Cincinnati: Hebrew Union College Press, 2001.

Baylis, Janice. *Sleep On It: The Practical Side of Dreaming*. Huntington Beach, CA: Sun, Man, Moon, 1977.

Book of Common Prayer (American Episcopal), The. New York: Seabury, 1977.

Brueggemann, Walter. "Holy Intrusion: The Power of Dreams in the Bible." *Christian Century* 122, no. 13 (June 28, 2005) 28–31.

Bulkeley, Kelly, ed. *Among All These Dreamers: Essays on Dreaming and Modern Society*. Albany: State University of New York Press, 1996.

———. *Dreams of Healing: Transforming Nightmares into Visions of Hope*. Mahwah, NJ: Paulist, 2003.

———. "Mystical Dreaming: Patterns in Form, Content, and Meaning." *Dreaming: Journal of the Association for the Study of Dreams* 19, no. 1 (March, 2009) 30–41.

———. *Spiritual Dreaming: A Cross-Cultural and Historical Journey*. Mahwah, NJ: Paulist, 1995.

———. *Visions of the Night*. Albany: State University of New York Press, 1999.

———. *The Wondering Brain*. New York: Routledge, 2005.

Bulkeley, Kelly, and Patricia Bulkley. *Dreaming beyond Death: A Guide to Pre-Death Dreams and Visions*. Boston: Beacon , 2005.

Bulkeley, Kelly, and Alan Siegal. *Dreamcatching: Every Parent's Guide to Exploring and Understanding Children's Dreams and Nightmares*. New York: Three Rivers, 1998.

Calvin, John. *Institutes of the Christian Religion*. Philadelphia: Westminster, 1960.

———. *John Calvin's Commentaries*. CD-ROM. Albany, OR: AGES Software, 1999.

Caprio, Betsy, and Tom M. Hedberg. *At a Dream Workshop*. New York: Paulist, 1987.

Chevalier, Jean, and Alain Gheerbrant. *The Penguin Dictionary of Symbols*. Translated by John Buchanan-Brown. London: Penguin, 1996.

Cirlot, J. E. *A Dictionary of Symbols*. Translated by Jack Sage. 2nd ed. Mineola, NY: Dover, 2002.

Coburn, John B. *Prayer and Personal Religion*. Philadelphia: Westminster, 1957.

Conforti, Michael. *Field, Form, and Fate: Patterns in Mind, Nature, and Psyche*. New Orleans: Spring Journal, 1999.

Cooper, J. C. *An Illustrated Encyclopedia of Traditional Symbols*. London: Thames & Hudson, 1978.

Crick, Francis, and Graeme Mitchison. "The Function of Dream Sleep." *Nature* 304 (July 1983) 111–14.

Davis, Patricia M. "The Weaning of Perpetua: Female Embodiment and Spiritual Growth Metaphor in the Dream of an Early Christian Martyr." *Dreaming* 15, no. 4 (Dec. 2005) 261–70.

Edinger, Edward F. *The Christian Archetype: A Jungian Commentary on the Life of Christ*. Toronto: Inner City, 1987.

————. *Ego and Archetype*. Baltimore: Penguin, 1973.

Edwards, Tilden. *Living in the Presence: Spiritual Exercises to Open Your Life to the Awareness of God*. San Francisco: HarperCollins, 1995.

Evagrius Ponticus. *The Praktikos and Chapters on Prayer*. Kalamazoo, MI: Cistercian, 1972.

Faraday, Ann. Introduction to *Dream Work: Techniques for Discovering the Creative Power in Dreams*, by Jeremy Taylor, 1–4. Mahwah, NJ: Paulist, 1983.

Fordham, Frieda. *An Introduction to Jung's Psychology*. 3rd ed. Harmondsworth, UK: Penguin, 1966.

Forest, Jim. *Praying with Icons*. Maryknoll, NY: Orbis, 1996.

Freud, Sigmund. *The Interpretation of Dreams*. Translated by A. A. Brill. New York: Barnes & Noble Classics, [1899] 2005.

————. *On Dreams*. Translated by James Strachey. New York: W. W. Norton & Co., 1952.

Gardenhire, Bob, and Carol Ludwig. "Dreams, Communing with the Divine: An Interview with Jeremy Taylor." *Presence: An International Journal of Spiritual Direction* 12, no. 1 (March 2006), 7–13.

Garfield, Patricia. *The Healing Power of Dreams*. New York: Simon & Schuster, 1991.

Gerona, Carla. *Night Journeys: The Power of Dreams in Transatlantic Quaker Culture*. Charlottesville: University of Virginia Press, 2004.

Hall, Calvin S. and Vernon J. Nordby. *A Primer of Jungian Psychology*. New York: Mentor, 1973.

Hobson, J. Allan. *The Dream Drugstore*. Cambridge: MIT Press, 2001.

————. *The Dreaming Brain: How the Brain Creates Both the Sense and the Nonsense of Dreams*. Scranton, PA: Basic, 1988.

Hoss, Robert J. *Dream Language: Self-Understanding through Imagery and Color*. Ashland, OR: Innersource, 2005.

Hudson, Joyce Rockwood. *Natural Spirituality: Recovering the Wisdom Tradition in Christianity*. Danielsville, GA: JRH, 2000.

Ignatius of Loyola. *The Spiritual Exercises and Selected Works*. Edited by George E. Ganss. Classics of Western Spirituality. Mahwah, NJ: Paulist, 1991.

Jenkins, David. *Dream RePlay: How to Transform Your Dream Life*. BookLocker.com, 2005.

Johnson, Ben. *95 Theses for the Church: Finding Direction Today*. Decatur, GA: Columbia Theological Seminary Press, 1995.

Johnson, Robert A. *Inner Work: Using Dreams and Active Imagination for Personal Growth.* San Francisco: Harper San Francisco, 1986.

―――. *Owning Your Own Shadow: Understanding the Dark Side of the Psyche.* San Francisco: Harper San Francisco, 1991.

Jung, Carl G. *The Basic Writings of Carl G. Jung.* Edited by Violet De Laszlo. New York: Modern Library, 1959.

―――. *Collected Works.* Vol. 8, *The Structure and Dynamics of the Psyche.* Translated by R. F. C. Hull. Edited by Herbert Read et al. Princeton: Bollingen, 1978.

―――. *Collected Works.* Vol. 9, Part 2, *Aion: Researches into the Phenomenology of the Self.* Translated by R. F. C. Hull. Edited by Herbert Read et al, Princeton: Bollingen, 1968.

―――. *Collected Works.* Vol. 11, *Psychology and Religion: West and East.* Translated by R. F. C. Hull. Edited by Herbert Read et al, Princeton: Bollingen, 1969.

―――. *Dreams.* Translated by R. F. C. Hull. Princeton: Bollingen, 1974.

―――. *Man and His Symbols.* With M.-L. von Franz et al. New York: Windfall/ Doubleday, 1964.

―――. *Memories, Dreams, Reflections.* Edited by Aniela Jaffé. Translated by Richard and Clara Winston. New York: Vintage, 1961.

Keizer, Garret. "Reasons to Join: In Defense of Organized Religion." *Christian Century* 125, no. 8 (April 22, 2008) 28–31.

Kelsey, Morton. *Dreams: A Way to Listen to God.* Mahwah, NJ: Paulist, 1978.

―――. *God, Dreams, and Revelation.* Rev. ed. Minneapolis: Augsburg, 1991.

Kidd, Sue Monk. *The Dance of the Dissident Daughter: A Woman's Journey from Christian Tradition to the Sacred Feminine.* San Francisco: HarperCollins, 1996.

Krippner, Stanley. Introduction to *Honoring the Dream: A Handbook for Dream Group Leaders,* by Justina Lasley, ix–x. Mount Pleasant, SC: DreamsWork, 2004.

Kuchan, Karen. "Visio Divina: Creating Sacred Space with Generation X." *Presence, An International Journal of Spiritual Direction* 12, no. 4 (Dec. 2006) 22–23.

Lasley, Justina. *Honoring the Dream: A Handbook for Dream Group Leaders.* Mount Pleasant, SC: DreamsWork, 2004.

Luther, Martin. *Luther's Works.* Edited by Jaroslav Pelikan. 54 vols. St. Louis: Concordia, 1955–1969.

Lyons, Tallulah. *Dream Prayers: Dreamwork as a Spiritual Path.* Smyrna, GA: Author, 2002.

Meier, Paul, and Robert Wise. *Windows of the Soul: A Look at Dreams and Their Meanings.* Nashville: Thomas Nelson, 1995.

Merrill, Nan C. *Psalms for Praying: An Invitation to Wholeness.* London: Continuum, 2005.

Moltmann, Jürgen. *God in Creation: A New Theology of Creation and the Spirit of God.* Minneapolis: Fortress, 1993.

―――. *The Source of Life: The Holy Spirit and the Theology of Life.* Minneapolis: Fortress, 1997.

Nelson, Geoff. "Benefits of a Parish Dream Group." In *Dreams and Spirituality; A Handbook for Ministry, Spiritual Direction and Counseling,* edited by Kate Adams et al., 182–91. London, UK: Canterbury, 2015.

―――. "Dreaming through the Bible with Luther and Calvin." In *Dreaming in Christianity and Islam: Culture, Conflict, and Creativity,* edited by Kelly Bulkeley et al., 57–70. Piscataway, NJ: Rutgers University Press, 2009.

Bibliography

Nouwen, Henri J. M. *Behold the Beauty of the Lord: Praying with Icons.* Notre Dame, IN: Ave Maria, 1987.

Opie, Iona, and Peter Opie, eds. *The Oxford Dictionary of Nursery Rhymes.* Oxford, UK: Oxford University Press, 1997.

Ott, E. Stanley. *Small Group Life: A Guide for Members and Leaders.* Decatur, GA: CTS, 1994.

Palmer, Parker. "The Clearness Committee: A Way of Discernment." *Weavings: A Journal of the Christian Spiritual Life* 3 (July/Aug. 1988) 37–40.

———. *A Hidden Wholeness: The Journey toward an Undivided Life.* San Francisco: Jossey-Bass, 2004.

Peterson, Eugene. *Working the Angles: The Shape of Pastoral Integrity.* Grand Rapids, MI: Wm. B. Eerdmans, 1987.

Pierce, Penny. *Dreams for Dummies: The Secrets of Dreams Unlocked!* Miniature Editions. Philadelphia: Running, 2001.

Presbyterian Church (U.S.A.). *The Constitution of the Presbyterian Church (U.S.A.): Part II, Book of Order, 2007–2009.* Louisville, KY: Office of the General Assembly, 2007.

Progoff, Ira. *Jung, Synchronicity, and Human Destiny: C. G. Jung's Theory of Meaningful Coincidence.* New York: Julian, 1973.

Rahner, Karl. *Theological Investigations.* Vol. 7. Translated by David Bourke. New York: Seabury, 1973.

Rycroft, Charles. *The Innocence of Dreams.* New York: Pantheon, 1979.

Sanford, John A. *Dreams: God's Forgotten Language.* New York: J. B. Lippincott, 1968.

Savary, Louis M., et al. *Dreams and Spiritual Growth.* Ramsey, NJ: Paulist, 1984.

Schwenck, Robert L. *Digging Deep: Penetrating Our Inner Selves through Dream Symbols.* Pecos, NM: Dove, 1979.

Singer, June. *Boundaries of the Soul: The Practice of Jung's Psychology.* Garden City, NY: Anchor/Doubleday, 1973.

Sobel, Mechal. *Teach Me Dreams: The Search for Self in the Revolutionary Era.* Princeton, NJ: Princeton University Press, 2000.

Strickling, Bonnelle Lewis. *Dreaming about the Divine.* SUNY Series in Dream Studies. Albany: State University of New York Press, 2007.

Swedenborg, Emanuel. *Heaven and Hell.* New York: Pillar, 1973.

———. *Swedenborg's Journal of Dreams, 1743–1744.* New York: Swedenborg Foundation, 1977.

Taylor, Jeremy. *Dream Work: Techniques for Discovering the Creative Power in Dreams.* Mahwah, NJ: Paulist, 1983.

———. "Dreams, Myths, and Social Justice." Talk presented at the International Association for the Study of Dreams Conference, June 25, 2005, Berkeley, CA.

———. *The Living Labyrinth: Exploring Universal Themes in Myths, Dreams, and the Symbolism of Waking Life.* Mahwah, NJ: Paulist, 1998.

———. Plenary Address. CD-ROM. Talk presented at the Spiritual Directors International 17th Annual Symposium and Conference, April 19–23, 2006, Costa Mesa, CA. El Cerrito, CA: Conference Recording Service, 2006.

———. *Where People Fly and Water Runs Uphill: Using Dreams to Tap the Wisdom of the Unconscious.* New York: Warner, 1992.

Tertullian. *The Ante-Nicene Fathers.* Edited by Alexander Roberts. Translated by James Donaldson and Arthur Cleveland Coxe. Vol. 3. Latin Christianity: Its Founder, Tertullian. Buffalo, NY: Christian Literature, 1885.

Tresidder, Jack. *Dictionary of Symbols*. San Francisco: Chronicle, 1997.

Tuoti, Frank X. *Why Not Be a Mystic?* New York: Crossroad, 1995.

Ulanov, Ann, and Barry Ulanov. *Primary Speech: A Psychology of Prayer*. Louisville, KY: Westminster John Knox, 1982.

Ullman, Montague. Introduction to *The Variety of Dream Experience: Expanding Our Ways of Working with Dreams*, edited by Montague Ullman and Claire Limmer, vii–xiv. Albany: State University of New York Press, 1999.

Ullman, Montague, and Claire Limmer, eds. *The Variety of Dream Experience: Expanding Our Ways of Working with Dreams*. Albany: State University of New York Press, 1999.

Van de Castle, Robert L. *Our Dreaming Mind*. New York: Ballantine, 1994.

Van Dusen, Wilson. *The Presence of Other Worlds: The Psychological and Spiritual Findings of Emanuel Swedenborg*. New York: Swedenborg Foundation, 1974.

Vennard, Jane E. *Praying with Body and Soul: A Way to Intimacy with God*. Minneapolis: Augsburg Fortress, 1998.

Waggoner, Robert G. "Does the Sailor Control the Sea?": Overcoming Resistance to Lucid Dreaming." *Electric Dreams* 13, no. 6 (June 2006) 23–25.

Ware, Corinne. *Connecting to God: Nurturing Spirituality through Small Groups*. Herndon, VA: Alban Institute, 1997.

Watson, David. *Called and Committed*. Wheaton, IL: Harold Shaw, 1982.

Watson, David Lowes. "Methodist Spirituality." In *Exploring Christian Spirituality: An Ecumenical Reader*, edited by Kenneth J. Collins, 172–213. Grand Rapids, MI: Baker, 2000.

Wickes, Frances G. *The Inner World of Childhood*. New York: Appleton-Century, 1966.

Wilkerson, Richard C. "John Herbert, Ph.D.: Online Dreamwork Pioneer." Dream Cyberphile. http://dreamgate.com/dream/cyberphile/cyberphile_19_4.htm.

Zimmerman, Nan. "After the Dream Is Over." In *The Variety of Dream Experience: Expanding Our Ways of Working with Dreams*, edited by Montague Ullman and Claire Limmer, 31–48. Albany: State University of New York Press, 1999.